# FORM AND PERFORMANCE

# ERWIN STEIN

# *Form and Performance*

WITH A FOREWORD BY
BENJAMIN BRITTEN

NEW YORK : LIMELIGHT EDITIONS
1989

*First Limelight Edition May 1989*

*Foreword © Benjamin Britten 1962*
*Text © Trustees of Erwin Stein 1962*

*Reprinted by arrangement with Faber and Faber*
*Limited.*

*Library of Congress Cataloging-in-Publication Data*
*Stein, Erwin, 1885-1958.*
*Form and performance.*
*Reprint. Originally published: New York : Knopf, 1962.*
*Includes index.*
*1. Music—Interpretation (Phrasing, dynamics, etc.)*
*2. Music—Performance.   3. Musical form.*
*I. Title.*
*MT75.S84   1989      780'.7'3        86-27744*
*ISBN 0-87910-061-3*

# NOTE BY LADY HAREWOOD

During the last years of his life, my father was engaged on this book. When he died in 1958 there remained two chapters still to be finished (on Tempo and Musical Architecture), but I felt that what he had written was too valuable not to be published. It was seen through the press by a group of friends—Benjamin Britten, Peter Pears, Donald Mitchell—and myself.

1961                                                    M.H.

# FOREWORD

### *by* BENJAMIN BRITTEN

Erwin Stein's name was known to a comparatively small circle of people. He himself was the last person to complain about this since his was a retiring nature and he believed (and how rightly!) that some of the most important work is done without the glare of publicity. There were occasions, however, such as that of a particularly execrable performance of one of his favourite works, when he would regret that he had not the chance to conduct more often; forgetting his natural modesty, he would say he 'could have shown them how!' And after reading this book one can easily believe that he was right, for it shows a rare gift for detailed analysis, and at the same time a warmth and understanding of the music which, in my experience, is unique.

He was not inexperienced as a conductor. Between 1910 and 1919 he conducted at many German opera houses and was responsible for the preparation of many different kinds of works, from the lightest to the most serious. Later he prepared and conducted the famous series of performances of *Pierrot lunaire* with Erika Wagner, first in Vienna and then touring across Europe to London. In the 'twenties he trained a chorus in Vienna and conducted Beethoven's ninth symphony. After he came to England, he only gave one public performance, that of *Pierrot lunaire*, at the Æolian Hall in 1943. Instead of conducting he listened, and so came to write this book. He listened to all kinds of musical performances with that devastating yet good-humoured criticism which was so characteristic: 'It was bad, of course', he might say, 'but not *so* bad.'

He could talk in fascinating detail of his early, and certainly his most important, listening experiences—those performances of operas and concerts conducted by Mahler in Vienna. He went to them with his friends Schoenberg, Zemlinsky, Webern, and Berg, and they would sit together for most of the night discussing what they had heard. It is from Mahler that Erwin learned most of the art of performance—the moulding of a work's form, a taut yet flexible rhythm, the balance of tone, sensitive phrasing, and intensity.

Although he was an admirer of Mahler's he never actually studied with him. He was however for some time a pupil of that great teacher Schoenberg. Erwin himself gave up writing music many years before he died (I never saw any of his compositions, and often wondered whether his critical faculty was not used too harshly on himself), but he was able to pass on much of the invaluable experience of his lessons with Schoenberg to young composers—whether they were his pupils or those with whom he dealt while acting as editor to two important publishing firms in Vienna and London.

Erwin's reaction to the new music one played him was never very quick. He needed time to assimilate it—the over-excited and inaccurate bangings to which he was subjected passed gently over him until he had had time to study the actual notes. And that to me is one of the most important things in this book—his insistence on the composer's actual notes, and on what lies behind them.

Those of his readers who are also performers may despair at the complicated task of following and carrying out such detailed advice; but they should not forget that after the intellect has finished work, the instinct must take over. In performance the analysis should be forgotten and the pieces played as if they were at that moment being composed. Although most of Erwin's work was done, as it were, behind the stage, he had the strongest understanding of those *on* it. He believed profoundly that one of the most important jobs in life was the communication of great musical truths, the truths he helps to reveal with such care and affection in this book.

# CONTENTS

9

# PREFACE

**B**ooks on performance are not written for posterity; it is the contemporary reader who is being addressed. The methods and manners of performance described in old treatises were not the custom of the day, but what the authors would have liked it to be; how music should have been performed, but, alas, was not. The situation has a counterpart in the recent spate of commentaries on performance of old music. Dissatisfied with its present-day performance, the commentators believe they know better and base their knowledge on treatises that were originally meant to teach past generations. It would be most gratifying if by this roundabout way better performances of old music could be secured than have ever taken place. But, unfortunately, the views of old writers often differ, and often contradict each other. It is not always easy to establish to which of the various schools of thought a piece of music belongs. We can learn a lot, if we read the books with discretion, but their reliability varies. If the author is a famous composer, his words have more authority than those of a mere theorist. Many problems must remain unsettled. The question of ornamentation, for example, can never be definitely decided, because ornaments were largely left to the taste and knowledge of people whose conceptions were very different from ours. Our minds have since absorbed another century or two—and what centuries! When all has been said, the truth remains that musical performance is less a matter of historical faithfulness, than of artistic sincerity.

The present book is written for my contemporaries. It is based, not on old treatises, but on the music itself. My subject is performance of music in our time. By music *in* our time

I have not only music *of* our time in mind, little though there has been written about its interpretation. Perhaps the detailed directions and expression marks in modern scores seem to make further explanations superfluous. And, it may be argued, the various means of recording the sound itself have made literary description obsolete. Records made by famous artists are easily available and more illuminating than words can be. However, the unavoidable vagueness of a verbal description seems to me a lesser evil than the confusion caused by some of the records. Students and future listeners are likely to be puzzled by the differences of interpretation—say, of a Beethoven symphony, conducted by Toscanini, by Weingartner, and by Furtwängler. If performances of the most famous artists vary in tempo and phrasing as much as the records, we must either allow for a freedom of interpretation not unlike the improvisations of the early musicians, or assume that unwarranted liberties have been taken. Discrepancies between performances are often a matter of different emphases; but often they are caused by misconceptions.

I do not underrate the examples of great performers. Gifted students can learn a great deal from them, but they sometimes accept their vices together with their virtues. *The details of performance have never systematically been investigated.* Nor do the customary analyses help the performer. At best they show that a phrase consists of motifs, that a movement is built of themes; they describe, perhaps, the course of a development or modulation. But they do not disclose why a certain melodic turn without a certain harmonic texture necessitates a certain amount of *rubato*; why a particular melody is most characteristic in a particular tempo, or why, and under what conditions, the term *tempo giusto* suffices to suggest the tempo the composer had in mind. We often feel that in the course of a piece a modification of the tempo or of dynamics is needed, but we do not know why. How much, and at what rate, a *ritardando* should slow down, an *accelerando* should speed up, a *crescendo* grow, a *diminuendo* abate; how long or short a *staccato*, a *tenuto*, a pause, should be—all these may be controversial questions, but in the end they are matters of form and proportions.

On such and similar details we find in the text of the music only more or less vague indications—if any. The intelligent musician is supposed to feel instinctively at what rate, and how loud or soft, the notes are meant to follow each other. But the intelligent musician often goes wrong. A sense of proportion is often lacking, especially as regards music's extension in time. It is a common mistake, committed by very famous artists, that undue prominence is given to certain passages, or even features of passages, to the neglect of others. A glaring example can often be heard in the last movement of Brahms' first symphony. At the start of the Allegro (*Allegro non troppo, ma con brio*), the tempo is usually taken too slowly and so is quite out of proportion to the movement's, and the theme's, character. The reason seems to be that conductor and violinists wish to indulge in the juicy sound of the G string. But the slow tempo unduly stretches the simple line of the melody. It cannot carry the over-emphasis imparted to it. To me, the theme heard in this fashion makes sound without sense.

Beauty of tone is a fine thing, but it is not the only quality to which the attribute of musical beauty applies. Musical sound is shaped, and beauty lies as much in the proportions of the shapes as in the physical phenomena of sounds. The average listener enjoys music's physical sensation. What he craves for is fulness of tone. The performer is tempted to supply in abundance what is most in demand, to the neglect of the formal proportions which, anyhow, only comparatively few listeners are capable of appreciating. But worse, it is the performers themselves who, with rare exceptions, vaguely feel rather than precisely understand the relations of the notes. If they knew, they would not tolerate the wrong accents that occur in almost every phrase. Almost every *ritardando* is a pitfall; those at the end of a piece almost invariably start too early, and slow down too quickly, so that the final notes become incoherent. A thoughtless method of performance prevails, which paralyses any sense of form a listener may possess.

If in this book I attempt to advise on musical performance, I am encouraged by the experience of a lifetime; but my authority is derived solely from the musical texts. The composer expresses his ideas by arranging the material of music in a certain order. The performer could not communicate the ideas if he did not strictly adhere to the composer's arrangement. The order of the notes, i.e., the form, must tell us how the music ought to be performed, but music is a complex thing and the notes delineate various formal features at the same time. Melody, harmony, texture, rhythm, dynamics and colour are the elements of musical form and, though they are inseparable and interdependent, in performance each of the elements as well as their mutual relations must be taken into account. For performance is a function of musical form.

Our investigations are meant to cover all types of music, vocal as well as instrumental. We shall consider the approach to music of the soloist, the member of an ensemble and the conductor. The principles of performance are the same for all, though similar ends often have to be achieved by different means. An adequate technique must, in this book, be taken for granted, but we shall distinguish between those instruments that can sustain notes and those, like the piano and harp, whose tone immediately subsides. Performers who produce the notes with the breath, the bow, or the hand, have to play, or sing, differently in order to phrase a melody alike. The conductor's task is comparable to that of the pianist, in that both are in control, not of a melody, but of an entire texture. And the singer has an additional medium to take care of—the words should not check, but promote the tone.

Our music examples are taken chiefly from music of the last 250 years. Some examples are analysed in great detail, but it would have exceeded the scope of the book if all important instances had been treated with the same thoroughness. This book is no more than a first attempt to deal with the problems of musical performance systematically and in a workmanlike fashion. If my method should prove successful, I sincerely hope that others will fill the gaps I have left, and correct such inconsistencies as have occurred.

# INTRODUCTION

Music consists of sounds, and the word 'form', applied to music, means the arrangements of sounds. *Per-formance*, then, is the realization of particular sounds in a particular order. The composer's imagination shapes the sounds; melodies, rhythms and harmonies are the terms in which he is thinking and the means of his expression. The impression on the listener, on the other hand, depends solely upon the manner in which the sounds are presented. The absolute supremacy of form is a consequence of the fact that music alone among the arts has no correlative in the world of our daily experience.

Of course, form is a basic feature in all the arts. Although the materials differ, their treatment shows certain analogies. Every artist wants to condense his imagination into a defined form. This is a prerequisite of any artistic communication, for our perception is subject to the order we discover in the perceived object. Every work of art, of whatever stuff it is made, has a distinct and distinctive form. The form is more than a quality or a framework. Rightly understood, it is the work of art itself. Let us be quite clear about that: *the act of artistic creation consists in the shaping of the material.* With the painter or the sculptor it is self-evident: let the picture before his mind's eye be as complete as it may, it is created while he paints the canvas, moulds the clay, hews the stone. The composer employs melodies, harmonies, rhythms, just as the painter, working in a different material, employs designs, colours, light and shade. However, the state in which the composer delivers his work is not the final state. Music must become sound to be real, and it is here that the performer comes in. The composer's score has been compared to the plan of an architect, both setting out neatly on a piece of paper what is meant to extend widely, the one in time, the other in space. Carrying the simile further, architecture has been described as frozen music; as if musical patterns, moving in time, were suddenly to become fixed and visible, revealing a single well-proportioned form. Both composer and architect must clearly conceive the shape of every detail and its bearing on all the others, and must balance beforehand the importance of the various parts in proportion to the whole. It would lead to disaster if the architect gave no due consideration to the qualities of the material, a neglect less perilous, but more frequent, in the other art. It happens only too often that a piece of music, ill-constructed by default of either the composer or the performer, tumbles down on the poor listener. Here the analogies end. Once the plan is carried out, the building is in existence for better or worse. Music, however, must be played or sung anew every time.

In poetry too some qualities are akin to music. Poetry can, though it need not, be translated into sound; language can be spoken or read, heard or seen. The division of time as a means of form is almost as important in the metre of poetry as in the rhythm of music. Inflexions of the speaking voice may amount to spoken melodies and impart to a recited poem an inkling of musical sound. The kinship of the two arts has created one of their finest flowers: the song. Yet their media are fundamentally different. However skilfully the poet applies the musical qualities of language, they remain secondary to the meaning of the words. The sounds of music depend for their sense on the way they are shaped.

Music has no other resources. The notes of which the simplest tune or the most elaborate symphony consists, are comprehensible only because they are ordered in a certain fashion, shaped into patterns that are repeated, juxtaposed, and varied, and built up into larger sections. The form is not a guise, but the very subject-matter of music. It is quite in keeping with this fact that the titles of many pieces indicate

18

their form, as Sonata, Fugue, Rondo; or an important formal feature, as Adagio, Quartet, Concerto.

The performer must have a crystal-clear conception of the music he is going to play, a conception which is necessarily in terms of sound. The better he understands the form, the clearer will be his conception. Form and sound must become identical in his mind. He ought to hear distinctly and vividly with his inner ear the exact shape of every passage, the extent of every *crescendo*, the accentuation of every phrase. It is not sufficient to rely on what he believes to be his knowledge of the music's emotional content. The purely emotional approach is bound to distort the proportions of the sound-forms.

Thus, the performer's first task is to put the notes together so that they make sense. They must cohere. Every note must have its place and meaning in the context, and each shape must be clearly designed. The succession or coincidence of the notes must sound logical and inevitable, each note having its due duration, no longer and no shorter, no louder and no softer.

Music is sound, and the sound must be clear, so that it can really be heard. The listener's faculty of perception sets limits to both quickness and slowness. Every rhythm needs a definite 'timing'—quite apart from the notes' values. If long notes are unduly drawn out, the music's continuity is interrupted; short notes lose their edge if they are not articulated. The quality of volume and colour depends largely on the allotted time. And also the clarity of successive notes is a matter of timing, while clarity of simultaneous notes is a problem of balance. It is here that the tasks of the conductor and the pianist (or for that matter of any keyboard player) are similar: both are in control of the entire texture. But the players and singers of orchestral and choral ensembles ought also to know the significance of their parts.[1]

[1] Unfortunately there are rarely sufficient rehearsals for new works and the players have little chance to learn what it is all about. As a result, composers are sometimes unjustly blamed for obscurity in their music.

Chords must be balanced, the features of both melody and accompaniment brought out, and polyphonic parts individually developed. Acoustic conditions must, of course, be taken into account. In an over-resonant place, say in a church, the performer may have to moderate the pace of a fast tempo and, perhaps, to increase the emphasis of details. Vivacity is not achieved by speed alone; on the contrary, the music becomes dull if it is played faster than its features allow. In vocal music, the distinctness of the words is a special problem, which we shall try to investigate.

The performer's paramount concern is to realize the character of the music; it is the purpose for which the music was written. He should not begin with preconceived ideas about moods or emotions to be expressed, but seek the character in the music's formal features. It is the structure of the music, resulting from its melodic, harmonic, rhythmical and dynamic components, that determines form and character at the same time. The character is given by the structure. In fully realizing the second he will convey the first, but by pulling the music about he will contort both. He must take account of the features of the structure and, in combining them, decide their precedence according to his sense of proportion and judgment of balance. To develop this sense and judgment is the purpose of this book.

The performer must aim at coherence, clarity and distinction of both the details and the whole of a piece. Maybe one feature will tempt him to a manner of performance that is unsuitable to another feature, and he has to draw a balance between contradictory claims. He should not delay the momentum of a theme in order to clarify, say, its harmonic structure; or ease the severe slowness of a *Grave* lest coherence might suffer. Clarity within a fast tempo is a matter of technique, coherence in a slow tempo depends upon the ability to keep the sound of sustained notes alive.

Many performers would have the necessary musicality and skill if they understood the implications of the musical structure. But, unfortunately, most of them are too preoccupied with points of technique to bother much about details of form. I well understand the craftsman's pride and his ambition to show his dexterity. For this there is ample opportunity in music, and not every opportunity is seized. Never should the performer allow his technique to interfere with musical form. Nor should he decide on any technical point, such as fingering, bowing and breathing, before he understands the phrase concerned.

The reader of this book is presumed to have a little knowledge of musical theory. I shall not explain the terms 'dominant' or 'sonata form'. On the other hand, I am starting from the very beginning, from music considered as an aural sensation. In analysing musical sound and its capacity for yielding palpable shapes, we shall become aware of the *elements* of which music consists. Combined, the *elements* go to form the *structure* of the music. Structural analysis will be our principal occupation, because the structure reveals the music's *character*. The performer realizes the character in a continuous *movement*, by *phrasing* the melody, focusing the *tempo*, and co-ordinating the sections of the form, so that its *architecture* is adequately balanced. Structural considerations cannot guarantee a good performance—this is a question of the performer's individual gifts—but will help to avoid a faulty one.

# I. THE ELEMENTS OF MUSICAL SOUND

*Das Ohr ist eines Musikers ganzer Verstand—*
SCHOENBERG

If, according to Schoenberg, a musician's intelligence rests in his ear, let us listen to the music we ourselves are making more critically than we are accustomed to. Quite at home as we are in the world of the eye, the realm of the ear is a fairly strange country. Before the eye things are firm and lasting, but to the ear everything seems loose and fleeting. Yet it is just these breaks and changes which make aural perception possible. If the sound remained unaltered, it would cease to be felt as a sensation. As light and shade disclose the outlines of a visible object, so the changes of sonority give shape to what we hear. As visible forms are confined in space, so, in the aural sphere, forms exist by their confinement in time, i.e., by the very limitation of their durations. Time is the dimension in which audible objects extend—but time is elusive. While we automatically relate visible objects to each other, aural impressions are felt as being connected only if they follow each other at short intervals. Take the sound of a bell: the strokes and the intervals between them mark the outlines of the sound, but the real thing is of course the sound itself, its timbre, whether sharp or dull, and its volume, whether loud or soft. In music, that extraordinary building erected in the space of time, the qualities of the sound are defined and organized. The infinite possibilities of timbre are restricted to a selected number of pitches—music's tonal aspect; the space of time —the temporal dimension—is divided into surveyable frac-

23

tions; and the volume of sound is harnessed into a graded scale of soft and loud dynamics.

Highly organized though music has been for many centuries, its notation has set almost insoluble problems. Among the components of musical sound it is only the pitch that is, as a rule, written as it is meant to sound.[1] But we know how different the notes sound with different players, even on the same instrument. It is not only timbre that makes for differences, but also methods of tone production, which, as a matter of technique, are outside the scope of this book. We shall do well, however, to recognize that each of the three methods of producing musical sound, by the breath, by bowing, and by the touch of the hand, has its intrinsic artistic merit. The breath is the most natural means of sustaining the notes and the one most directly under the control of the mind, once the performer has attained technical breath control. The arm which handles the bow has more flexibility but less steadiness than the breath. The touch of the hand yields less variety of colour, but is by nature more articulate than either arm or breath. The performer ought to be aware of such qualities and deficiencies, in order to cultivate the one and to overcome the others.

Music ranges over a ladder of eight to nine octaves, but the distinction between low and high notes is relative to the compass of the passage and of the instrument on which it is being performed. The open G string of the violin is a very high note on the double bass; and the high register of a tenor voice, which according to popular appreciation yields some of music's brightest and most brilliant sounds, is within the more or less indifferent middle register of a soprano voice. Whether a note is felt to be high or low does not only depend upon its pitch, but also upon its colour. The act of producing the highest or lowest note, on the voice as well as on many instruments, contributes to its character of brightness or darkness.

[1] This is to be taken with a grain of salt. Pitch has changed very greatly in different epochs and different places.

As for music's temporal dimension, the written values of the notes indicate their durations relative to each other, while metronome figures (e.g., $\dot{\textstyle\int}$ = 100, i.e., a hundred crotchets to the minute) measure their absolute durations. But both note values and metronome marks are only approximately accurate. Crotchets and quavers are not to be taken at their face value; nor do metronomical figures suggest that every minim must last exactly as long as another. The duration of the notes is subject to their meaning in the context. The result is an infinite diversity of time-patterns, which go to form short rhythmic motifs or larger rhythmically defined structures. The distinction between long and short notes is as relative as that between low and high pitch —it is all a question of relations and proportions.

Pitch and duration are the basic factors of musical sound. As regards pitch, the notes represent the substance of the music—its body, as it were; music's extension in time, on the other hand, marks its outlines. But it is not so much the actual duration of notes, as the succession of articulations that determine the rhythm. Lack of sustaining power has not prevented the piano and its forerunners from becoming popular instruments. Their short-lived tone has been the source of a special style in which sustained notes are replaced by figures, arpeggios and ornaments. There was a time when the ornamentation of long notes had become an accepted rule; C. P. E. Bach, in his *Versuch über die wahre Art das Klavier zu spielen*, 1753,[1] wrote, 'Singers and performers on instruments that are not defective in this respect' (of sustaining the notes), 'also do not dare to deliver an undecorated note for fear of eliciting only bored yawns.' (W. J. Mitchell's translation, part I, p. 150.) Later composers, especially Chopin, Liszt and Debussy, showed great ingenuity in turning the deficiencies of the piano into virtues, by developing a texture appropriate to the instrument. Performers ought to distinguish between figurations that

[1] Translated and edited by W. J. Mitchell and published as *Essay on the True Art of playing Keyboard Instruments* (Cassell, 1951).

replace the sound of sustained notes and those that constitute a genuinely quick movement.

The volume of tone, i.e., the degree of loudness or soft-
ness, contributes less to musical structure than pitch and
duration, but is an essential means of presenting the music
clearly. If one considers music's infinite shades of *p* and *f*,
the notation of dynamics is very vague. No valid measurement has so far been established. The exact meaning of
dynamic signs or the degree of loudness to which a *crescendo*
should grow must be gathered from the context. The fact
that the dynamic range and the capacity of increasing or
decreasing the tone volume widely differs with different
instruments, adds to the responsibility of the performer.

Apart from the pitch, duration and volume of the notes,
there are the elements of timbre and colour, which contribute to musical form in various ways, though their constructive power is relatively small. Timbre and colour are
often used synonymously, because both are caused by the
amount and quality of overtones and resonances the sounding medium produces. But we shall distinguish in this book
between the timbre, proper to a specific instrument or voice,
and the colour caused by its individual treatment. The
timbre is given by the scoring: the colour is sometimes indicated as a special manner of execution, e.g., *pizzicato*, harmonics, soft pedal, *con sordino*. Beyond such more or less
exact indications, the intended effect is sometimes hinted at
by technically undefined expression marks, such as *dolce*,
which leaves the choice to the performer of how to achieve
the requisite sweetness. Mostly, however, the colour is not
described but implied in the music's character.

The singer has, by way of the words, an additional means
of colouring the notes. In singing, the words are an integral
part of the music: vowels and consonants are musical sounds
and parts of the voice's colour.

Not that the elements of sound can be isolated: they
always appear as an entity. While the pitch is noted in con-
stant values, the indicated duration as well as dynamics and

colour are variable within a narrow margin. Their variability is the source of a multitude of expression marks, which, as the word signifies, indicate the aim rather than the means, i.e., the character of the intended sound rather than the sound itself. Terms like *espressivo, rubato, energico, marcato* refer to several musical elements at the same time. Their interpretation by different performers shows how interdependent the variable elements are. A *rubato*, for instance, may have a function similar to an *espressivo*; the increase and decrease of volume connected with an *espressivo* may, under certain circumstances, replace the rythmical freedom of a *rubato*; or, if the performer applies both *rubato* and *espressivo* at the same time, he needs less of either: less deviation from the indicated note values, and less dynamic shading. Relevant examples will be given; for the moment it must suffice that length, strength and colour of the notes are the performer's principal means of shaping the form.

# II. THE ELEMENTS OF
# MUSICAL FORM

## 1. *The Tonal Aspect*

The form of music consists of the order of its component parts which, in the last analysis, includes the arrangement of the elements of musical sound: pitch, duration, volume and colour. Notes of different pitch go to form melodies if they follow each other, chords if they sound simultaneously. A melody is an ordered succession of notes. Though in every melody the rhythmic element is included, we shall at first consider the tonal component; for the shape of the melodic line is the first thing the performer has to take account of. Two principles of order can be distinguished: the direction of the line and the size of its intervals. Both the direction—upwards, downwards, or alternatingly both ways, i.e., in zigzag—and the intervals are significant features.

We distinguish between conjunct and disjunct motion, conjunct motion progressing in steps, disjunct motion in leaps.

The theme of Mozart's G minor symphony, K.550, centres on the leap of a sixth.

Mozart, Symphony No. 40 in G minor, K550, 1st mvt.

We recognize the line's direction upwards in disjunct motion and, subsequently, downwards in conjunct motion. Whether, and by what means, the performer should emphasize the features of the line, will be discussed in a wider context. In general, simple shapes need less emphasis than complex ones. Within the narrow scope of a melodic line a step is simpler than a leap, and a frequent change of direction more complex than a straight scale. The highest and the lowest notes of a melody are, as the orders of its compass, important points of which the performer must be aware. Melodies with a large compass, or which include wide leaps, are commonly felt to be emotionally expressive.

*J. S. Bach, St. Matthew Passion, Evangelist*

The widely ranging zigzag line of the recitative from the *St. Matthew Passion* is suggestively descriptive of the dramatic event.

The more uncommon and surprising an interval, the greater is its significance. In Beethoven's piano sonata, Op. 111, the huge leaps that lead from the bridge passage to the second subject are the climax of the sonata's exposition.

That leaps are felt to be more expressive than conjunct motion is a firmly rooted musical convention, whose source is probably the exertion needed for connecting widely separated notes.

If notes are merely repeated, it goes without saying that

Beethoven, Sonata No. 32 in C minor, Op. III, 1st mvt.

the rhythm is more significant than the 'line'. Unfortunately it is a bad habit of string players and clarinettists not sufficiently to articulate, but to blur, the rhythm of repeated notes, especially if they are within a passage of *legato* character. A fraction of a second's rest is needed between them or else they will sound as one note.

Many melodies, especially of classical composers, are based on familiar chords. We need not assume that lack of melodic inventiveness is the reason; but the well-known tonal relations impart to the melody, though in disjunct motion, a character of obviousness and assuredness. If Beethoven chooses to use a melody that looks like an arpeggio figure as the principal theme of his *Eroica*, he wants it to be played nimbly, as his own metronome figure indicates.

Beethoven, Symphony No. 3 in E flat, Op. 55, 1st mvt.

Pompously to inflate the theme is against both the letter of 𝅗𝅥.= 60 and the spirit of the simple line.

Repeated chordal figurations without thematic significance almost invariably denote that the melodic line is not the most essential feature of the particular musical structure. In the first prelude of Bach's *Forty-Eight* the arpeggio melody cannot be misunderstood, but the harmonic progression of changing chords constitutes the form of the piece and must be made comprehensible. Therefore, the melody needs no emphasis; the tempo, on the other hand, must be sufficiently fluent, so that the listener can grasp the connections and modulations of the chords.

**J. S. Bach, The Well-Tempered Clavier, Book I, Prelude No. I in C**

The principal features of any chord are the number of its notes and the quality of its intervals. While the number of notes goes to form the texture of the chord, the quality of its intervals makes the chord a consonance or a dissonance; the meaning of the term dissonance, however, has changed through the ages. The dissonance of yesterday has often turned into the consonance of today and the once fundamental distinction between them has become relative to the context in which they figure. Schoenberg, in his *Harmonielehre*, bases his definition upon the overtone series, when he describes consonances as near and simple relations, dissonances as more remote and complex relations between the notes. The difference is, in fact, one of degree. In the midst of triads a chord may be a dissonance, which among complex chords may sound like a consonance. Dissonances are not an outstanding event in music in which consonances are the exception.

31

C. P. E. Bach wrote:[1] 'Dissonances are played loudly, consonances softly.'—'An exceptional turn of the melody which is designed to create a violent effect must be played loudly.' —'A rule which is not without foundation is that all notes of a melody which lie outside the key may well be emphasized, whether they form consonances or dissonances, and those which lie within the key may be effectively performed *piano*, again regardless of consonances or dissonances.' These must have been admirable rules for the performers of his time, though sometimes the composer provides the necessary emphasis by other features of the passage, e.g., rhythm or texture, in which case anything the performer adds is an over-emphasis—a very frequent error. On the other hand, where dissonances prevail and melodies are more 'outside the key' than inside, different and more subtle methods of performance will be needed.

Chords enrich the sound and, very likely, this was their original purpose. But the sounding together of different notes raised formal problems of great complexity, which the composers of many centuries have solved in different ways. It was during the epoch of modal music that tonality and harmony in the modern sense gradually emerged. With the masters of polyphony, harmony was the relationship not between chords, but between simultaneous melodies.[2] Harmony, as expressed in chords, gained prominence after the tempered scale had been established and eventually became an almost independent province in the realm of music. As for the performer, he need not unduly worry about the period to which a work belongs. Styles of performance vary, not because a work was written at a certain date, but because works of certain periods have certain features in common. Not a preconceived style, but features of the melody, harmony and texture teach us the reasons why we must phrase Scarlatti differently from Debussy.

[1] Op. cit.

[2] Herein rests, I believe, the difference between Rameau's and Bach's conceptions of harmony.

THE TONAL ASPECT

The term 'tonality' in the broadest sense refers to any interrelations of notes with regard to their pitch (in this sense we speak of the tonal aspect of musical form). Tonality in the narrower sense, i.e., tonality centred round a tonic, prevails in the bulk of the music which is the performer's daily fare. Within the major and minor keys, the harmonic relations and functions are closely defined, all chords and implied harmonies gravitating towards the tonic. The graded affinities to the tonic of the degrees of the major and the minor (dominant, subdominant, submediant, mediant and supertonic), the relationships of the keys based on these affinities, and the chromatic chords derived from the key relations, amount to a thorough organization of tonal harmony. Bach's rich harmonic structures are already the acme of organized perfection. In Mozart's harmony chromatic chords are by no means rare. While in Verdi's operas the vocal melody is all-important and the harmony is relatively simple, the opposite is the case in Wagner's music: the harmony is very complex and the melody less developed—in fact, the harmony often takes the first place. It is Wagner more than any other composer, whose harmonic sophistication and inclusion of the remotest and most alien chromatic chords broke through the boundaries between the keys. The strict rules for the use of dissonances have always been flouted by the best composers, but the *emancipation of the dissonance*, as Schoenberg calls the freedom with which it is used today, has been made possible by the diminished power of the tonic. Still, it depends upon the composer whether he employs the means of harmony for establishing a key, or not. And we have not lost the feeling for the subtle grades of tonal relations in which classical music excels.

The minor mode includes more chords than the major, in that two different triads exist for each of its degrees; and even the tonic often tends to become a major triad at the end. The resulting ambiguity gives the minor mode a wide harmonic scope that already in Bach's music occasionally borders on what we call today bitonality. On the other hand,

33

there is a great affinity to the relative major whose tonic easily gains supremacy and whose key often dominates the subsidiary sections of pieces in the minor. More interesting still are parallel keys, because their relationship makes for the intrusion into the major of chords from the minor (such as the minor subdominant, the diminished seventh and the Neapolitan sixth), thus widening the scope of the key. The vacillation between the major and the minor, the mood changing with the mode, gives some of Schubert's pieces the character of waywardness. Mahler's music, too, abounds in abrupt juxtapositions of the two modes.

*Mahler, Symphony No. 6, 1st mvt·*

The word *harmony* is often used as a synonym of *chord*, but our musical vocabulary will be more correct if we apply the term not to single chords, but to the relations between them, and also to certain aspects of the melodic line.[1]

While on the one hand the function of the leading note is self-evident, every note of the diatonic scale is related to the five other degrees as well as to the tonic. An implied harmony, though often ambiguous, is one of the significant features of a melody. The performer must be aware

[1] I believe that in music without a tonic centre, including compositions with twelve notes, harmony also operates through the relations of the notes. Chords refer to the *basic set* (Schoenberg's English term for his German *Reihe*), and the evaluation of chords will have to take into account the constitution of the set (i.e., its intervals) and its application to the particular work. There are no rules—each case is a special one.

whether the line is diatonic or chromatic, and whether it forms a cadence or a modulation. Elaborate chromaticism within a key needs careful phrasing.

*Mozart, Rondo in A minor, K.511*

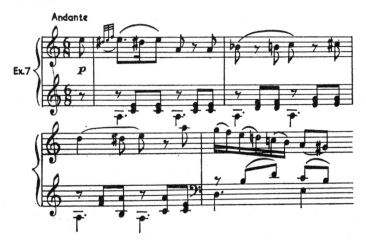

In Mozart's A minor Rondo, the notes of the second and third bars are not just chromatic passing notes, but component parts of chromatic chords. To 'play them loudly', according to C. P. E. Bach's recipe, would impair the balance of the melody. Perhaps the expression *armonioso* is the best description of how the relevant chords should sound: the notes of both strands must be equally distinct. The rising thirds of the left hand are an essential feature of the texture: if they are heard, the harmony will be clear.

Although the formative power of harmony is very great, it is in general the design and rhythm of the melody that determine the character of the music. However, there are instances in which the harmony is more important than the melody. In the development sections of sonata form and similar schemes, the modulations and the sequence of keys are more significant than the sequential repetitions of themes which by this time have become well known to the listener. And there are passages in music of the nineteenth and twentieth centuries in which harmony is more significant than melody.

Wagner, Tristan und Isolde, *Prelude, 1st act*

Wagner, Siegfried, *Erda Motive, 3rd act*

In the examples from Wagner's *Tristan* and *Siegfried* it is the suggestive power of the harmony that imposes its character upon a melodic line which itself is not very strongly characterized.

We are accustomed to speak, by way of metaphor, of music's horizontal and vertical dimensions, the horizontal referring to the succession of notes, the vertical to their sounding at the same time. Together the horizontal and vertical extensions go to form the texture of the music, which may be homophonic or polyphonic. The texture consists of at least two strands, and may comprise many more.

In homophonic music one strand carries the principal part while the others are subsidiary—the accompanied song is the prototype. Often in orchestral and keyboard music there are no distinct strands and the number of parts changes freely. In polyphonic music the strands are of more or less equal importance. They move independently of each other, in that their melodic lines and rhythms do not coincide. But the independence is, of course, not absolute. In a canon the parts depend upon each other, though they do not coincide.

Confusion of the terms chord and harmony has been the source of an erroneous distinction between harmony and polyphony. They are not opposite principles. It is quite true that thinking in terms of chords does not produce polyphony. A succession of chords, ornamented by passing notes, suspensions, etc., makes for a pseudo-polyphonic texture. In polyphonic music the parts are the principal thing, but harmony is inevitably involved. Harmonic functions are expressed in the movement of parts, not in an underlying, implied chordal scheme.

Complex textures pose difficult problems to the performer. He must aim at lucidity and transparency in both polyphonic and homophonic music alike, and must be fully aware not only of the principal part, but also of the character and function of the other strands. Treble and bass are prominent by nature, because top and bottom, the outlines of the texture, fall most easily on the ear. But the melody is not always on top. In a fugue, the successive entries of the theme should not obscure the other parts. It is wrong to over-emphasize the main point at the expense of secondary points. In homophonic music too, the accompanying and subsidiary parts must be properly worked out. The performer will do well to treat homophonic textures not so very differently from polyphonic ones, by giving each strand or chord its individual character. Even short entries in ensembles, which contribute only a few notes to the common cause, should be played audibly, if discreetly. Good ensemble textures result from good team work.

37

## 2. *The Temporal Aspect*

### (A) TIME AND RHYTHM

Music extends in time, and a span of time filled with music is a real thing, as defined and organized as a sculpture is in space. In order to become a concrete reality, however, music must be performed. The performer shapes the music as the sculptor moulds the clay. In music, time is divided, but a piece of music is a whole. The notes are particles of time which cohere through their palpable relations. And what we call *rhythm* is the palpable relation of notes to their duration. A rhythm comprises two or more notes, and, in a wider sense, rhythm applies to the temporal proportions of the notes. The ear recognizes the order of the note-values as they pass by and distinguishes the groups that they form. Rhythm organizes music's temporal dimension. It marks the outlines and is in consequence the most conspicuous musical feature. But these outlines are too flexible for exact notation. Note-values are only approximately correct. They provide a scheme from which the rhythm can be inferred. In fact, the rhythm has to be supplied by the performer.

Time as a musical term has a special and limited meaning: it divides music's temporal dimension arithmetically. The time-signatures systematize the relations of the note-values, and the bar lines facilitate the reading of the music. We learn that there is a strong beat at the beginning of, and lesser or weak beats within, a bar. The regularity, however, which the time-signature suggests, and the symmetry which the note-values imply, is more often latent than apparent in live music—and often non-existent. Strong beats are not always required; sometimes the first note is not a strong, but a long one, not accentuated, but sustained (*tenuto*); and sometimes the first beat is not emphasized at all. There is a difference between an accent and a *tenuto*; the first has dynamic, the second rhythmic significance. For the sake of

clear distinction, we shall call the rhythmic emphasis provided by a prolongation of the note a *stress*, and shall use the
term *accent* for indicating a dynamic emphasis. Accents
sometimes support the rhythm, but are often employed on
purely dynamic grounds.[1]

Time provides a common denominator for the changes of
rhythm, but we should be aware that the terms time and
rhythm represent opposing principles. Time means absolute
strictness, rhythm relative freedom; time arranges the notes
into groups of equal duration, while the rhythmic particles
are of different lengths; time counts the note-values, but
rhythm depends upon other features of musical form. Once
we understand the relations of the notes, we find that the
values and bar lines, which at first reading have been help-
ful, lose the meaning of exactitude. The value of every note
is modified by the structure of the phrase and the place of
the note within it. A degree of *rubato* is needed in almost
any kind of music, and certainly in any melody of defined
shape, though the application must vary in different styles.
In Bach's music the *rubato* will often be hardly perceptible
if compared with the flexibility appropriate to a melody by
Chopin. Yet in both instances the principle that the duration of the notes is determined by their meaning within the
context is valid. I have termed *rubato obbligato* the slight
deviations from the arithmetical note-values, which musical
sense, i.e., musical form, necessitates.

Time unifies the diversity of rhythm. Every quaver may
have a different duration, but the differences amount rarely
to more than a fraction of a split second. Though the deviations are so small that the pulse of the time remains to be

[1] The term metre belongs to poetry and spreads confusion if applied
to music. The quantity of syllables bears no comparison to the time-
value of notes; and musical rhythm is more diversified than metrical
schemes. Recitation invests the verse with more flexibility than the
rigid metre shows, but the reciter's rhythmical freedom, his *rubato* as
it were, is derived from the meaning of the words, while the performer's rhythmical inflexions are—or should be—attributable solely
to the musical form.

felt, they are vital—their neglect inevitably dulls the music. In any case, the performer is accustomed to working with split seconds; the twentieth part of a second is not too short for a note within a run, and a whole second is a long time. Here is a theme that takes just under four seconds:

Beethoven, *String Quartet in D, Op. 18, No. 3, 1st mvt.*

Roughly speaking, our understanding of rhythm depends upon a clear appraisal of what distinguishes long notes from short ones. It is not only a difference of degree but of kind. The chief significance of long notes rests in their dynamics and colour. They stand out by nature and must therefore be kept in audible proportion to the short ones. As far as technique is concerned, long notes pose problems of execution which differ with different instruments. Sustained notes are occasions where the performer can show his individual resourcefulness. Sometimes a sustained note requires a certain amount of inflexion of dynamics and colour in order to preserve the continuity of a phrase. Uninflected sustained notes are still more difficult to keep alive. The player has to maintain the act of tone production without flagging. Its density and intensity must uninterruptedly be renewed and controlled. Smooth, concentrated tone results from a continuous stream of breath, or continuously even pressure of the bow on the string, whatever the dynamics. Instruments like the piano, which have no way of renewing the tone, must resort to faked sustaining by means of richer texture or pedalling, greater fulness of the sustained note or by clipping its duration. The good performer imparts to the note that degree of intensity which makes one feel, directly he strikes the note, how long it is going to last.

The significance of short notes is chiefly melodic and rhythmical. They must be clearly articulated in order to be understood and the last, especially, of a succession of fast notes must remain distinct, even if it stands at the end of a *diminuendo*. Voices and instruments which are not very articulate by nature must enunciate the notes particularly carefully and, if necessary, take more than the allotted time—a possible reason for a *rubato obbligato*. Clear articulation achieves distinct rhythm (without accents) by hitting the exact pitch at the right moment within the correct degree of dynamics.

There is a limit to the shortness of notes: the sound becomes percussive if the ear has no time to perceive the pitch. I recently heard a recording of the *Eroica* with the staccatos of the first two chords so short that the common chord of E flat was hardly perceptible—a glaring defect in the performance.

Dotted rhythms ( ♩. ♪ or ♩.. ♪) in which the second note is only a fraction of the first are apt to cause a moment of rhythmical tension that ought not to be overtaxed. The first note should not be so long drawn out that the tension relaxes before the second is heard; or be so short that the second becomes meaningless. In one word, the relation between notes of different length must be understandable.

An upbeat is closely connected with the succeeding note— the bar line is no barrier. The basic form of an upbeat is short–long ( ♪ ♩) as opposed to the dotted rhythm long–short ( ♩. ♪ ). The context must decide whether the short note should be linked with the preceding or the following note. In triple time, rhythms derived from the scheme ♩. ♪♩ almost invariably signify that the short, second, note should be attached to the third. Strangely enough, we do not find the distinction between the two different rhythms in old text-books. On the contrary, C. P. E. Bach writes: 'The short notes which follow dots are always made shorter than the written text indicates' (transl. A. Dolmetsch). The author is a great authority, but we feel old music differently today, and the invariable shortening of the note after a dot sounds to us mannered. There are many instances in his father's works in which we do not prolong the dot—rightly I believe—but preserve the indicated note-value, e.g., in the ritornello and accompaniment of the E flat major contralto aria from the *St. Matthew Passion*; though we shorten,

**J. S. Bach**, St. Matthew Passion, *contralto aria in E flat*

or should shorten, the semiquaver of the choral call 'Wohin?' because it is an upbeat. Upbeats of an evocative character, e.g., in *largo* introductions, are to be shortened, not only in old, but often in new music too. But upbeats that are part of a motif which is to be developed, should be treated differently, according to the merits of each case.

Syncopations break the system of the indicated time, in that the weak beats are emphasized at the expense of the strong ones. That the strong beat is both less accentuated and less stressed than the weak is the basic principle, but many, and more complex, designs are derived from this scheme. Syncopations provide rhythmic contrasts within a melody (cf. Ex. 30, p. 76) or between the strands of a texture (cf. Ex. 65, p. 132).

Syncopations in an accompaniment have sometimes little rhythmic significance and need not be sharply articulated. They replace, as it were, sustained notes and keep the tone alive, especially on the piano.

A syncopation is felt as such only if the pulse of the regular time remains in being or is somehow implied in the rhythm. In the trio from Schubert's *Moment Musical* in

*Schubert*, Moment Musical *in C sharp minor, Op. 94, No. 4 trio*

C sharp minor, the weak beats are not only stressed but also accentuated, and this circumstance makes it indispensable that

THE ELEMENTS OF MUSICAL FORM

the performer should feel distinctly—and not cease to feel —the latent 2/4 time; otherwise the music will sound as in Example 13.

*Legato* closely connects the notes without any break between them. The term 'slur' for the curved *legato*-line suggests that no distinct articulation of the notes is wanted; *legatissimo*, in fact, 'slurs' the transitions between the notes. Nevertheless, the pitch of each should be clearly recognizable from the start. *Portamento* is a special manner of playing, by which the sliding from one note to the other is made audible. Not wholly avoidable where large intervals are to be connected, *portamento* should be restricted to the minimum possible. The (wrongly) so-called *glissando* of the strings and the 'scooping' of the voice are for the most part bad mannerisms, and caused by lack of technique.

A note is not as a rule sustained until the next begins, but I believe that C. P. E. Bach over-simplifies the case when he writes:[1] 'Notes that are neither staccato nor legato are to be played for half their value, except if the word tenuto is added, in which case they must be sustained.' Not only between *staccato* and *non legato* notes, but also between those that are played *tenuto*, there are gaps—unwritten rests— whose duration must be controlled. Whether and how much the notes should be detached from each other depends upon the structure of the phrase. The breath of the wind player and singer is in general a more spontaneous and precise regulator of a note's duration than the bow, which often remains on the string when it should be lifted. But it need not be so. String players who are really in control of their bow, ought to be capable of mixing at will any short and long notes in any rhythmical combination.

In sustaining a note there are many degrees between *legato* and *staccato*. *Tenuto* ⸀(‐) means usually that the note should be held almost as long as its value indicates, robbed only of the minute particle that is needed for preparing the articulation of the next note. The sign ⸏ usually shows that

[1] Op. cit.

the note is to be sustained and yet distinctly separated from the following. The duration of notes that are 'neither staccato nor legato' is determined by the context in which they appear, and may often approach the character of a kind of long *staccato*.

*Staccato* indicates that the note is short, but there are many degrees of shortness, especially in slow tempo. Artur Schnabel, asked by a pupil whether he should play a passage *staccato*, replied: 'Which *staccato* do you mean, No. 7 or No. 56?' Great laxity prevails in the performance of *staccatos*, especially among orchestral players—and here conductors too are to blame. No difference is made between dots over crotchets and quavers, and almost any note that ends a phrase is too short. The length of *staccato* is often decisive for the character of a phrase, and always for the brilliance of a passage, but few performers know subtler distinctions than *staccato* and *staccatissimo*. Many connect with the notion a quality of explosiveness that is not in its nature, unless the *staccato* is also marked *marcato*. Here is a field that needs cultivation. *Staccato* playing is a touchstone of both a performer's musicality and technique.

Today, composers are fairly explicit in writing out in full the rhythm of passages whose correct execution would formerly have been taken for granted. Mozart, for instance, writes the second subject of his string quartet in E flat major thus:

*Mozart, String Quartet in E flat, K.428, 1st mvt.*

There can be little doubt that the note-values were meant to sound differently—probably thus:

In Schoenberg's *Serenade*, op. 24, similar rests are written out in full.

*Schoenberg, Serenade, Op. 24, 1st mvt.*

The first two rests make for *staccatissimo*; the third is a phrasing rest; the fourth is both a phrasing rest and *staccato*; the fifth indicates that the preceding note is detached; and the sixth makes for *staccatissimo*, like the first.

Rests should be taken at their exact arithmetical value as rarely as the notes. Their duration depends on the function they fulfil within the structure and, in particular, on whether the rest is meant to create a moment of tension or relaxation—if relaxation, the value will tend to be prolonged; if tension, it will tend to be shortened. Rests serve as punctuation marks and separate, but also join, the phrases. The performer will best fulfil this double function of separating and connecting, if he keenly feels, rather than exactly counts, the appropriate time interval. Perfect rhythm does not depend on the values of either notes or rests.

Rests are part of the musical structure and sometimes as full of meaning as the notes. Within a phrase, they serve the clear definition of rhythmic shapes. The hesitating rests within the melody of Chopin's *Nocturne*, Ex. 35 (cf. Chapter III, p. 81), are rhythmically important and intensify an expression of sadness. And the rapid alternation of violent chords and rests in the first movement of the *Eroica* amount

Beethoven, Symphony No. 3 in E flat, Op. 55, 1st mvt.

Allegro con brio

to abrupt contrasts of loudness and stillness—flashes of light, as it were, that are the more blinding for the intermittent darknesses.

## (B) TEMPO

We are told that in past times the tempo was indicated by combinations of note-values and time-signatures. It was a sound method as far as it went, but one that gave only approximations. Our note-values indicate relative durations, while the tempo, which determines the absolute duration of the notes, is quite a different problem. The tempo, the rate at which the music proceeds, provides the frame for the display of musical events. Not only the rhythmic proportions but also those of the other elements must find in it their proper measure. The tempo is a coalition of variable factors and will miscarry if each element is not properly gauged; for each of them, rhythm, melody, harmony, texture, and dynamics, needs its own kind of clear and coherent delivery. Together, the elements form the structure of the music, in which the composer has embodied the music's character.

47

Tempo is a function of the structure. It must allow the music to sound characteristic—in fact, it is the character that is indicated in most of the traditional tempo indications. Roughly speaking, the distinction is between slow and fast tempi. And, roughly, slow makes for clarity, fast for coherence. Nothing should pass too quickly for the listener's comprehension, nor too slowly for absorbing his undivided attention. In either case the form would be out of focus: if the tempo is too quick, the notes become blurred, if too slow they lose coherence. In general, developed structures need a slower exposition than simple and straightforward ones. The traditional middle movements of the symphony and sonata are cases in point. The scherzo, derived from dance forms, usually goes quickly ahead with simple designs; in slow movements on the other hand, the melodies are rich and abound in variations.

The distinction between fast and slow is sometimes deceptive. The apparent speed depends less upon the rate at which the notes follow each other than upon the character of the rhythm. You can play very fast without agitation; and slow but energetic rhythms can make a very vivid impression.

The tempo is one of the performer's most important means for holding the form together, and should make a piece of music, in spite of contrasting characters and moods, a well-balanced whole. The same tempo, *l'istesso tempo*, should therefore be maintained. But this rule must be rightly understood. Maintenance of the same tempo provides unity, but should not curtail the music's diversity. *L'istesso tempo* does not exclude *tempo rubato*. There is an old rule of thumb for performing *rubatos*: an acceleration should be counterbalanced by a subsequent retardation, and *vice versa*, thus making up for the fractions of time gained or lost. We have it from two distinguished witnesses, Mozart father and son, that *rubato* should not change the tempo. Leopold Mozart, in his *Violin School*, warns the accompanist not to yield to the soloist, 'he would only spoil the tempo rubato'. And Wolfgang writes in a letter, 'That I always accurately keep time, makes them all wonder. The tempo rubato in an adagio—that the left hand does not know about it, is what they cannot understand; with them the left hand gives way.'

To maintain the same tempo throughout an extended piece is a difficult task. Tempo bears upon the character of the music but if there are several themes of different characters, a tempo has to be found that is apt to all. *Rubato obbligato* allows for a certain latitude and will thus ease the problem; a second theme can, perhaps, be played, say, at the quickest pace to which an earlier *rubato* has accelerated. Unity is preserved if the first tempo is reintroduced. Such modification as is necessary should be slight—insensible as it were—giving the impression of *l'istesso tempo*; *quasi l'istesso tempo* is the term for it. But definite changes of tempo should only take place where they are indicated. It will not do to begin Beethoven's piano concerto in G major, for example, dreamily and slowly, leaving an embarrassed conductor with no choice but to play the *tutti* of the orchestra in a different tempo. No, the call of the piano and the answer of the orchestra must cohere.

*Beethoven, Piano Concerto No. 4 in G, Op. 58, 1st mvt.*

49

The *rubato obbligato*, inherent in the melody's repeated quavers, makes the theme sufficiently flexible to permit a slight broadening in the fourth bar; but the sustained opening chord of the phrase and its last bar must be well in time.

A temporary increase or decrease of the basic speed, i.e., *accelerando* or *ritardando* with subsequent *a tempo*, is a *rubato* on a large scale. The tempo is so characteristic a quality and so memorable that our sense of proportion is satisfied if the first rate of movement returns.

*Accelerandos* and *ritardandos* which are meant to lead to a new tempo are a different affair. Here, the performer's task is not quickly to reach another tempo, but to spread the change evenly throughout the passage. It may be a good thing to introduce, along the lines of *tempo rubato*, the terms *tempo accelerando* and *tempo rallentando*. There are *accelerandos* that do not end with the establishment of a new tempo. The first movement of Mahler's first symphony accelerates throughout the exposition and again during the recapitulation, to the end of the movement. And in Berg's opera *Lulu* there is a scene during which the tempo quadruples its speed within 160 bars, from *Grave* to *Prestissimo*, and then slows down again to the initial *Grave*.

The measurement of tempo has always proved difficult. Any method must suffer from the relativity of the notions fast and slow. I believe that words describing the character such as *vivace, con fuoco, grazioso, cantabile*, are more suggestive than mere reference to the speed. Mixed terms, indicating both the speed and the character, often with warnings added, such as *non troppo, quasi, poco*, and *assai*, bear, unfortunately, a different significance in the work of almost every composer; and at different periods of his life the composer will feel differently about the character the terms are supposed to convey. The use of other languages than the traditional Italian completes the confusion, but happily it is only a confusion of terms. The structure of the music to which they refer implies the tempo and discloses the meaning of the terms. The tempo is born with the music, while the tempo indication is not. Composers often have to think twice before they find the appropriate expression. They often change tempo indications and metronome marks, and sometimes even the time-signature and notation. Mozart began the finale of his string quartet in B flat, K.458, in *alla breve* time before he decided that a

*Mozart, String Quartet in B flat, K.458, 4th mvt., discarded version*

lighter character, suggested by 2/4 time and marked *Allegro assai* instead of *Prestissimo*, was more adequate.

In search of an exact measurement the idea emerged of comparing a succession of beats with the pulse of the human heart. It is a nice idea, but as a method hardly controllable. Richard Strauss once thought it 'probable that the pulse of the present generation beats faster than it did in the age of the postchaise'. However, human nature does not change as quickly as that. We have proof that Berg, who I think belongs to the present generation rather than to the postchaise age, and J. J. Quantz, who belonged to that age, both considered the same rate of pulse-beats to be the normal one. Quantz suggests that tempo should be measured by the average pulse that beats about eighty times a minute; and Berg wrote on the top of the song that is the centre-piece of his opera *Lulu*, 'In the tempo of the pulse beat, ♩ = 80 .'

When Mälzel constructed the metronome, Beethoven was among the musicians who enthusiastically greeted the invention. It was then that he added metronome figures to all his symphonies, to his string quartets, up to op. 95, and to a few other works. But later he abandoned the attempt to metronomize his works because he discovered that the figures were not really consistent. The metronome is arithmetically exact, but musical rhythm is not. While verbal tempo indications are vague, metronome marks are rigid. Reger metronomized the progress of extended *ritardandos*, but one cannot metronomize the subtleties of a *rubato obbligato*. The metronome fixes only one—the note-value —of a number of quantities that are variable and interdependent. The other quantities belong to the sphere of phrasing, and include, apart from *rubato*, unwritten rests, stresses, accents, and inflexions of dynamics and colour. The balance between the tempo and the other features is most delicate. Rhythm and dynamics influence the movement and can set a metronomically correct tempo out of focus. A tempo that deviates to a degree from the metronome figure is preferable to one that blurs the musical design. And there are many structures that allow for a certain latitude of tempo.

The usefulness of metronome figures has often been questioned. Wagner metronomized his early operas, but found that the method was no safeguard against grave mistakes. Each time he complained about a wrong tempo, the conductor claimed that he had observed Wagner's markings,[1] and who could disprove him after the event? Many figures in current editions of nineteenth-century music are questionable, because it is difficult to assess whether they are the composer's or an editor's. We do not know whether the problematic metronome figures in Schumann's music are his own or Clara Schumann's.

In our time, metronome figures have become a generally accepted method of fixing the tempo. Stravinsky gives sometimes no other than metronomical tempo indications, while Bartók indicates every section of a movement in minutes and seconds. But paradoxically the exact observation of the figures does not guarantee the right tempo: too strict an obedience dulls the music. Schoenberg says in his scores: 'Metronomical figures are not to be taken verbally, but only as a guide' (*Andeutung*). A famous conductor once confessed that he never looked at the figures; yet his tempi are convincing because he realizes the musical structure. We must approach metronome figures as we do verbal tempo indications. They cannot guarantee, but can help to find, the tempo. The best method of metronomizing is, not to try and fix the note-values of the first bar, but to establish the average rate of movement with the help of a stopwatch. The figure found will not exactly correspond with every beat and may be wrong even for the first bar, but the intelligent performer will understand that this is due to *rubato obbligato*.

The most important single factor is the rhythm: the tempo gives it its *Lebensraum*. The note-values must attain their inherent proportions, with the long notes just so long, and the short ones just so short, that their sequence makes coherent sense. Finally, the performer must take the

[1] Richard Wagner, *Über das Dirigieren* (*On Conducting*).

character of the music into account and decide on a tempo that sets the musical object sharply into focus.

The performer makes up his mind before he begins, and feels the responsibility of his decision. If the tempo is wrong, everything is distorted. A remedy after a false start is difficult and will leave a blemish. It happens all too often that a tempo must perforce be changed, in passages that blatantly expose the initial mistake. The picture of sound which the performer imagines before his mind's ear ought to be so well defined that its very clarity compels him to the right tempo. But there are performances in which the player's arms or fingers rather than his mind dictate the speed. And any tempo indication is useless if the performer does not understand the music.

## 3. *Dynamics*

The varying degrees of tone volume constitute the dynamics. Their scope is wide, but we face difficulties if we try to fix a graded scale between *fff* and *ppp*. There is no such thing as an absolute *p* or *f*. Dynamics are relative to the power of instruments and voices: an *ff* on a flute is hardly louder than a *p* on a trombone. The dynamic range as well as the capacity of increasing and diminishing the volume of tone differs not only with different instruments but also with their registers. Within the extremes, however, of the loudest and softest possible notes the degrees of dynamic shades are practically unlimited: their subtlety depends upon the performer's skill. In modern orchestral scores the dynamic marks for the instruments are usually differentiated, but in classical scores they are uniform. Every trumpet player knows that he has to restrain his *f* in a Haydn symphony; it is not the *f* of the trumpet that is meant, but the *f* of the ensemble. On the modern piano, the middle and bass registers have much wider dynamic range than the treble, and the pianist must balance the texture accordingly, especially of old keyboard music.

Dynamics do not yield to as thorough an organization as pitch and time, but contribute to musical form in various ways. Dynamic contrasts have always been used for sharply outlining the form, e.g., by way of juxtaposing solo and tutti, or by the soft echo of a repeat. The notation of detailed dynamics is a fairly recent practice; up to Bach's time we rarely find any indication, and even Mozart is not always explicit. The appropriate degree of differentiation which the performer should apply depends upon the features of the structure, i.e., on what we are accustomed to call the style of the music. Owing to its structure, the music of Bach needs broad dynamic outlines and few changes, which are, in general, restricted to contrasts or graded increases and decreases on a large scale.

The exploitation of dynamic gradation coincided with the development of both the piano and the orchestra. When the pianoforte arrived, its name must have had a ring of triumph for contemporary musicians; at long last there was a keyboard instrument with an almost unlimited dynamic range! We know that Beethoven indulged in juxtaposing *pp* and *ff* contrasts. Haydn and Mozart reserved them for rare occasions, such as the sudden *ff* on the word 'light' ('and there was light' in the *Creation*), the 'surprise' in the famous symphony, or the entrance of the ghost in *Don Giovanni*. Elsewhere dynamic contrasts were mostly between *p* and *f*. On the other hand, from their elaborate *cantabile* melodies, it appears that both Haydn and Mozart were conversant with a great subtlety of dynamic shades, which, if not always indicated, are implied. When Mozart speaks of the 'rubato in an adagio' which his listeners admired, we may be sure that the *rubato* involved very subtle dynamics. As for vocal music, inflexions of both dynamics and rhythm are in the very nature of singing. Soloists are accustomed to freedom of delivery, but often transgress the proportions of musical form.

The formative power of dynamics rests in the enormous possibilities of graded contrasts, which set the form into relief and support the architecture. By contrasting soft and loud 'terraces of sound' the sections of a piece are distinctly grouped. The gradual increase of tone volume—the extended *crescendo*—is perhaps the most conspicuous among dynamic features. Sometimes a dynamic climax carries the burden of the form—examples abound since Beethoven (fifth symphony, *Egmont* overture, etc.), and there are pieces, such as the preludes to *Lohengrin* and *Tristan,* whose architectural plan is based on dynamic gradation. The double *crescendo* on the note B in the third act of Berg's opera *Wozzeck* makes sense both as form and as dramatic expression.

The gradual decrease of tone volume is by nature less conspicuous; nevertheless, *diminuendos* have an important place in musical architecture. Many pieces end with the sound dying away—there is no need for examples.

Dynamics on a small scale serve to shade the melodic design, to accentuate the rhythm, and balance or differentiate the strands of the texture. Not all the notes of a phrase have exactly the same volume of tone, even if they are on one dynamic level. Slight dynamic differentiations add to

Beethoven, Symphony No. 2 in D, Op. 36, 2nd mvt.

the coherence of a phrase. The subtle gradation of dynamics, and especially graded accentuation, is a means of phrasing and as such as important as the stresses and *rubatos* of rhythm. Within every group of notes there is one that is its melodic centre. It need not be the highest, longest, or loudest of the notes, but it is usually emphasized by a rhythmical stress or dynamic accent however slight. Phrasing consists not only in separating or joining the phrases, but also in shaping rhythm and dynamics around the melodic centre.

A sudden drop of the dynamic level need not disrupt the coherence of a melody any more than a sudden increase. In Ex. 21 the melody centres, in spite of the dynamics, on the first beat of the third bar (the melodic apex), and the *appoggiatura* should perhaps not be stressed, but certainly not neglected. The melodic centre of Ex. 22 coincides with the

*Mozart, Violin Concerto in D, K.218, 1st mvt.*

last note of the phrase, the crotchet G, on which the rhythm comes to rest and the harmony reaches the root position of the dominant seventh chord.

A distinction between dynamic and rhythmic features cannot always have been clearly drawn. Many a *sf* has rhythmic significance and implies a *tenuto*; many a *rubato* needs dynamic inflexions. And clear articulation can be produced either by rhythmic or dynamic means. The articulation of a note necessitates its separation from the preceding one, which in non-*legato* is a rhythmic feature; in *legato* phrases, however, which are by nature less articulate, distinct articulation is hardly possible without a slight accent.

Music's formal elements are interdependent and their relationship is subject to too many variable factors to permit exact classification. Certain rules that have been formulated oversimplify the facts and performers will go astray if they believe that a rise of the melody always involves an increase, a fall a decrease of dynamics; or that a progression from the tonic to the dominant is a *crescendo*, and from the dominant to the tonic a *diminuendo*. There are many reasons for *crescendos* and *diminuendos*. A descending melodic line may represent a climax, and the cadence to the tonic may be its culmination. Dynamic differentiations can clarify musical structures, but their application is subject to other formal features and can only be based on the merits of the case.

Not every note is a *fp*; today this truism needs to be stressed, because the cultivation of the pianoforte (it would have been better named the forte-piano) has led to an utterly wrong conception of sound. The tone of the piano rapidly diminishes immediately the key is struck: thus every note is a *fp*, or at any rate a *marcato-diminuendo*. Unfortunately, the conception of the sound of the piano has influenced many players of those instruments which are capable of sustaining the notes. We can hear violinists, and even singers, who 'play the piano' on their fiddles or throats by stressing the articulation of every note. The dynamics of the piano are problematic; genuine only if the notes move quickly, they have cunningly to be faked if longer notes occur. The player is compelled to replace the lack of sustaining power by artifices of his touch, which colour, balance or spread the notes. Pianists are very skilful in suggesting a wide and subtle dynamic range by merely hinting at it. A melodic *crescendo* is produced by a *crescendo* of articulations, with the pedal perhaps delaying the inevitable *diminuendos*. Although this type of dynamics is not really satisfactory, we accept it as a convention. C. P. E. Bach refers to similar cases when he writes:[1] 'There are many things in music which are not really heard, but must be imagined.' And he gracefully continues: 'Intelligent listeners replace such deficiencies by their imagination, and it is chiefly this type of listener whom we like to please.'

The principal distinction is between *p* and *f*, while *pp* describes a softer *p*, and *ff* a louder *f*. Most of the subtle dynamic grades are shades between *pp* and *f*. There is one degree that is wrongly applied more often by performers than indicated by composers, and much abused: *mf* is usually, in effect, a *p* that is too loud, and sometimes an *f* that is too soft. Performers indulge in *mf* in order to give the sound sufficient 'body', but the music loses distinction because *mf* thickens the sound and obscures the texture; it makes for the opposite of transparency, which is a musical texture's most excellent quality. The indication *mp* is comparatively rare, but more useful than *mf*, especially for marking the principal part of a soft polyphonic passage. The restraint, implied in the expression *mp*, makes for a more distinguished sound than *mf*. Most *mf*s could be replaced by *mp*s with little infringement of the text and much advantage to clarity of the sound.

An *ff* is not always just a louder grade of *f*. The *ff* character is sometimes born with the music and immediately apparent from its structure. The best example that springs to my mind is the movement called *Der Siegesbogen* ('Triumphal Arch') from Schumann's Fantasia in C major. The *ff* character of the principal theme is obvious from its melody and texture, though, paradoxically, the dynamic indication is at first *mf*—obviously a technical point of dynamic economy. The indication *fff* on the other hand, can hardly mean anything else than an unusually loud *ff*.

Within the soft regions of dynamics, *pp* has a great variety of meanings. It is not only a dynamic feature, but represents a character of sound suggestive of tender, mysterious or uncanny expression—we need only remind our-

[1] Op. Cit.

59

selves of the grave-digging scene from *Fidelio*: *pp* is likely to increase the dramatic tension by straining the listener's attention. Soft dynamics contribute to transparency of the texture, and *pp* is the most cautious type among them in that it keeps every possible grade of dynamic power in reserve. The performer should be capable of the widest dynamic range that his instrument or voice permits, and be well aware of his own individual dynamic scale from the softest to the loudest notes. A wide range is needed both for the graded contrasts of the architecture and the subtle points of phrasing. The basis of musical sound is the *p*. Every performer should be conscious of how he sounds when playing *p-ordinario*, and certain other degrees should form landmarks in the field of dynamics: his own *f-ordinario*, his own *pp* and *ff*. Fixed dynamic levels help to secure gradations between them.

The expression *sotto voce* ('under the voice') is not a term of dynamics but of colour, and means 'with restrained sonority'. Otherwise, a relative maximum of sonority is understood, even in *p* or *pp*.

'*Crescendo* means *piano*, *diminuendo* means *forte*'— Hans von Bülow's paradoxical formulation should make memorable what is really a rule of thumb: it should prevent the widespread habit of playing loudly immediately a *crescendo* is in sight, and playing softly immediately a *diminuendo* appears. Both increases and decreases should be evenly spread across the passage to which they apply. *Crescendo* and *diminuendo* are gradual changes of dynamics, just as *accelerando* and *ritardando* are gradual changes of tempo.

Accents are subject to dynamic proportions; it is the relative, not the absolute loudness that counts. The notation of accents is still less settled than that of other dynamic features, and there is considerable confusion about the significance of *marcato*, $>$, $\wedge$, *sf*, *fp*, etc., because the practice of composers varies, even during their life. In general, we can distinguish three types of accents:

60

(1) *Marcato* (*marc.*, >, ∧) indicates an accentuated articulation. It is a feature not only of accentuation, but also of melodic emphasis. The sign ∧ is less common than > and usually indicates a heavier *marcato* which slightly prolongs the accent. Schoenberg introduced two signs of metrical scansion, ⌐ and ∪ , the first indicating that a note is to be stressed like a strong beat, the second that it should be dropped like a weak beat. These marks, however, apply to rhythm rather than to dynamics.

(2) In present usage, *sforzato* (*sf*, *fz*) indicates a sharp accent that stands out forcefully from its surroundings. It is a purely dynamic feature whose loudness is relative to the context, even if it is *sff*. *Sforzatos* are often exaggerated, or neglected, by performers, and composers would do well to accept Stravinsky's method of indicating the dynamic level: *sf in pp*, or *marc. in p*.

(3) *Fp* indicates a short but distinct *f*, which recedes to *p*. The short *forte* is the chief feature; whether the transition to the *piano* is abrupt (*p subito*) or a rapid *diminuendo* must be gathered from the context.

There is no clear-cut distinction between the three types of accents, and the one may occasionally replace the other. Their formal function is to clarify the texture by emphasizing important notes or strands. The tutti-sound of an orchestra can often be made transparent by *fp* for the brass instruments only, while the other players sustain the *f* level. In this way, the weaker instruments are distinctly heard and the *f* character of the passage is preserved, in spite of the *fp*.

Dynamic marks are sometimes used for indicating the rhythm, as in the finale of Mozart's string quartet in D minor (K.421). In the second variation, the first and second violins are at cross purposes with the time-signature, 6/8. Every fourth quaver of the first violin is marked *fp*, thus suggesting 3/8, while *fp*s in different places suggest 12/16 for the second violin. It is not the dynamics, the contrasts between *f* and *p*, that are to be emphasized. It is the cross

61

*Mozart, String Quartet in D minor, K.421, 4th mvt.*

rhythms of the violins that must be phrased distinctly, that is, independently.

Our notation (23) shows the polyrhythmic structure of the variation. In Mozart's score (24) the violins are written in 6/8.

The quality of any texture depends almost entirely upon dynamic balance. It makes for a cleaner sound if the principal part is set into relief, not by louder dynamics, but by softer playing of the subsidiary parts. In *p*, there is more scope for characterization, by rhythmical as well as dynamic means. And clarity in polyphonic music is best achieved by individual phrasing of each strand. The signs ᚼ and ᚾ which Schoenberg introduced, should be understood in this sense, ᚼ meaning 'principal part' (*Hauptstimme*), ᚾ 'subordinate part' (*Nebenstimme*): (1) the subordinate part should be softer than the principal part, (2) both should be phrased individually, though the principal part more elaborately.

Owing to their lack of precise notation, dynamics are largely at the player's discretion. Unfortunately those indications which are marked are often not sufficiently observed. It is a very common mistake of performers to play too loudly. *Pianissimo* is more difficult and more exacting than *mezzoforte*, especially if the tempo is fast. Apprehension that their indications will not be sufficiently regarded, induces composers sometimes to exaggerate their demands. Sometimes dynamic marks amount to warnings rather than exact directions; in any case, the performer has to gauge their meaning from the proportions of the musical structure.

## 4. *Timbre and Colour*

Timbre is a quality of musical sound which contributes only indirectly to musical form. The selected timbres of the orchestra and the organ stops constitute nothing like a system. Like dynamics, timbre is a means of supporting other formal features, especially useful for emphasizing the contrast of juxtaposed phrases or for setting the strands of polyphonic textures into relief. For such purposes any choice of markedly different timbres is suitable.

The timbre of an instrument or voice is the specific character of its sound; colours, on the other hand, are produced by inflexions of the timbre. The term colour is taken from the visual sphere, but musical colour is not as defined a means of construction as the colours on the painter's palette. Reedy or smooth, dark or bright colours, open or closed vowels, are only a few very rough distinctions within a wide range of tints and shades. The composer indicates the timbre by the scoring, but for describing the colour he has little other means than vague expression marks. He must rely on the performer's ability to understand and realize his intentions, which are implied in the structure of the music. In colouring the timbre the performer has a comparatively wide margin for interpreting the text—in fact, the individual colour that he applies is a performer's legitimate vehicle for expressing his own personality.

To have a wide range of colour at his disposal is a most valuable, but rare, gift. Imagination as well as skill is needed for conceiving and realizing the appropriate shade of every passage. The gifted performer, who hears the shades of colour clearly with his inner ear, makes the fingers, bow, lips, or breath unfailingly obey his demands. The possibilities of colouring the timbres are very great, and many artists could exploit their instruments to better purpose than they usually do. Among pianists, the ambition to increase velocity and volume of tone has almost degenerated into a race as to who can play the fastest and loudest. They had better try to extend their technique in other ways that are as important, if less glamorous. They should practise playing slowly and softly—slowly, but preserving continuity of sound; softly, but with sonority; they should cultivate a great variety of *staccatos*, which are necessary for sensitive phrasing; and they should develop the faculty of colouring the sound.

The methods of colouring the timbre differ with different

instruments. In applying, say, the expression mark *dolce* the composer demands a 'sweet' colour, which the pianist produces by a soft touch and cautious pedalling; on a string instrument, a similar type of colour is a matter of fingering, bowing and *vibrato*; while with wind instruments the evenness and roundness of the notes depends chiefly on the lips and the breath. The short sound of notes on the piano seems not to allow for much variety of colour, but the skilful pianist works wonders with his touch, by balancing the texture and by imaginative pedalling. More than anything else, it is the all-pervading *mezzoforte* that dulls the sound.

The different manners of playing the *string instruments*—*pizzicato, con sordino, sul ponticello, sul tasto, col legno*, and harmonics—amount not only to so many different timbres, but, with a skilful player, to many more different colours. In addition, the different timbres of the strings, the fingering, the density and amplitude of the *vibrato*, the speed of the stroke and the variety of bowings, not to mention the various *staccatos* and *spiccatos*, provide an inexhaustible source of colour variety. Complete control of the bow is an indispensable condition for exploiting these rich resources—but it is a condition which, unfortunately, not many players are capable of fulfilling.

Among the wind, the flute has not much variety of colour; its virtues are steady notes and easy movement. If flute players would try to increase their dynamic range and practise playing *crescendos*, *pp* in all registers, and *ff* in the middle range, they would at the same time gain a greater variety of colour.

The reedy sound of the oboe makes for a clear definition of the notes. Good players are capable of very subtly graded *crescendos* and *diminuendos*. The oboe is by nature 'expressive', and the same can be said of the English horn, though its notes are less articulate. There is no other instrument of the orchestra that yields as willingly to neat phrasing as the oboe. On the other hand, the 'expressiveness' tends to make the sound unsteady and oboists should therefore aim at the strictest breath control, which will also increase their limited dynamic range. Players should cultivate sonority of the highest register, a steady *p* of the lowest notes, and a variety of *staccatos*, especially at high speed.

The clarinet, by virtue of its greater compass, velocity and dynamic range, has certain advantages not possessed by the oboe, but its sound is less defined and the intonation less sure. Clarinettists should practise clear articulation of *staccato* and *staccatissimo*, especially in the middle and low registers, and try to extend the characters of the various registers to the whole compass, thus assuring, with the bass clarinet added, consistent colours through almost five octaves.

The notes of the bassoon are steady, and the timbre, by nature somewhat vague, gains increased distinction in quick movement and disjunct motion. Bassoon players should practise velocity in *staccato* (the finale of Beethoven's fourth symphony!) to improve their articulation, and should aim at increasing their dynamic range, especially in *crescendo*.

Brass instruments excel in brilliance of colour, dynamic power, and steadiness of tone. Owing to its great compass and comparatively easy movement, the horn is the most versatile among them, but its articulation on the *p* level is very delicate and needs continual cultivation. All brass instruments, especially the trombones, should cultivate *staccato* and *staccatissimo* playing. The timbre of the muted brass is not only characteristic, but blends well with the woodwind; however, the notes lack both volume and clear articulation. Trumpet players are accustomed to the mute, but the other instruments too could surely acquire a greater variety of dynamic grades than is commonly heard?

A change of dynamics almost invariably involves a change of colour, because with the increase or decrease of tone certain ingredients of the timbre become more audible, or less. It is up to the player's individual skill to maintain the same shade of colour in spite of different dynamic degrees.

The singer must, like the instrumentalist, aim at variety

of colour, but limitations, or rather definite directions, are imposed on him by the words. The idiom 'setting words to music' gives a very superficial idea of what the composer does: he combines music and words to form a unity. The words with their vowels and consonants are part and parcel of the musical sound: they are the very vehicle of the colour and should not hinder, but promote, tone production. Vowels have different timbres which the singer should colour, not only in accord with the sense of the words, but also in accord with the character of the musical phrase. In a good song the two features will fall into line.

The musical function of the consonants is very different from those of the vowels. Initial consonants are a means of articulating the notes (as if struck on the piano), though triple consonants will sometimes delay the articulation. Consonants in the middle or at the end of a word are likely to cause an inflexion of a preceding short vowel. Within a *legato* phrase, consonants should smoothly join the notes. An explosive consonant at the end of a phrase should not be pronounced as an appendage to the music. Crossing of the *t*'s, in which German Wagner-singers indulge, is hardly appropriate to vocal style, because it infringes the melodic line. The inclusion of explosive consonants into musical sound is a difficult item in the singer's tone production. The natural inflexion, particularly of a vowel or continuant that precedes a mute consonant, makes it possible to hint at, rather than distinctly to articulate, the explosive sound. In *non legato* phrases such consonants may aptly be fitted into the little gaps between the notes. The words will clearly come across if they are allowed to be part of the music, with each vowel and consonant contributing its particular colour.

Colour is not only an element of the melodic line, but also an important component of both homophonic and polyphonic textures; and it is here less the inflexions of timbres, than the spacing, movement, dynamics, and balance of the strands that make the colour. Chords, in particular, represent distinct characters, whose colour is sometimes more

67

significant than their harmonic function. Colour is conspicuous in Debussy's music and often the principal feature of the musical structure. In his piano prelude *La terrasse des audiences du clair de lune* (cf. Ex. 60), the colour and texture of the chords suggest the character of the music, which is enhanced by *pp*-dynamics and, to a lesser degree, by the design of the melody and rhythm. In the third of Schoenberg's *Five Orchestral Pieces*, Op. 16, the colour of a sustained chord keeps changing, in that its notes are taken by different instruments in succession. The composer attempts to realize an idea which he mentions on the last page of his *Harmonielehre*; if our ear could discriminate between shades of colour as distinctly as between differences of pitch, it might be feasible to invent melodies that are built of colours.

Another constructive use of timbre occurs in an orchestral arrangement by Anton Webern of Bach's six-part *Fuga Ricercata* from *Das musikalische Opfer* (*The Musical Offering*). By distributing small motivic particles between instruments of different timbre, the melodic structure of the theme is made to stand out in relief.

Bach, orch. Webern, Musical Offering, *Fuga Ricercata* (*six parts*)

# III. STRUCTURE

The composer gives his ideas defined form by shaping and organizing the material of music. The performer reproduces that form in order to convey the composer's ideas, but he will fail in his task if he does not understand how the form is organized. A piece of music is a composite whole whose component parts have different lengths. The order in which the large sections are arranged constitutes what we shall call the architecture. At present we are concerned with smaller sections that are sufficiently homogeneous immediately to be felt as units. They may comprise a single phrase, a fully organized melody or theme, or the developed pattern of a transition.

Within these units music is organized in various degrees of complexity. The formal elements, combined, go to form the structure of the music, which includes: the design of the melody and its harmonic implications (cf. Chapter II, pp. 28–38), harmony itself, the vertical and horizontal texture, the rhythmic shapes and rhythmic groupings—symmetrical or otherwise—and significant features of dynamics and timbre.

There are, it follows, various structural aspects: the structure of a melody is given by its line and rhythm; the structure of harmony by the tonal relations of notes and chords; the rhythmic structure by the grouping of phrases; the structure of any passage by the sum and balance of its melodic, rhythmic, harmonic and textural features, and—as far as they are of structural significance—by the features of dynamics and timbre.

## THE VARIABLE FEATURES

Roughly speaking, the structure is revealed by the graph

of the music, but some of its features are variable (cf. Chapter I, pp. 26–27). Rhythmic deviations from the arithmetical note-value and subtle shades of dynamics and colour are conditioned by—because they are—functions of the structure. The variable values of rhythm, dynamics and timbre are interdependent. A *rubato*, for instance, may require dynamic inflexions, a *tenuto* an inflexion of colour. The distinction between the structure and its variable functions is vital for a good performance. The features of the structure disclose how its variable components are to be applied. To give them their adequate emphasis and in the right proportions is, after the delivery of the text, the performer's chief responsibility. If he understands the structure, he will phrase sensibly, distribute correct accents and stresses, and properly balance the texture. The structure reveals the character of the music. Structure and character are different aspects of the work of art, but the performer's approach to a piece should be by way of the structure.

The performer has a certain margin in his application of the variable components, but the scope is not very wide, for the proportions depend, on the one hand, upon the arrangement of the fixed components, and on the other hand, upon the rate of the listener's perception. It is not just a question of how quickly the listener's mind can follow—or how slowly—without missing the context. Our ability to understand the music while it is being performed depends upon the performer's ability to convey the meaning, and this in the last resort depends upon his sense of form and timing.

### BEGINNING

Musical form consists in the order of its component parts, and musical structure consists in their relations. The possible combinations of music's formal elements are inexhaustible, but certain principles are inherent in any musical form by its very nature. The beginning of a piece of music is abrupt; seemingly without relevant cause it begins from nowhere. Music gains shape while it continues, but the first impulse is decisive in setting the stage and pace of the subsequent events. Every performer knows the high degree of concentration that he needs in order to have at the start and at a moment's notice a whole piece of music in a nutshell in his mind. He is embarking on a venture from which, once begun, there is no escape. While he performs, he is nothing but the music.

The abruptness of an opening may be lessened by various means. Often there is the ceremony of an introduction which prepares for the things to come. A slow introductory section may raise a sense of expectation and may contrast with a subsequent quick movement. Sometimes there are only a few preparatory bars which evoke the atmosphere of the piece; sometimes, more elaborately, the music gains shape gradually with particles of a theme slowly emerging until its full stature is announced—the opening of the *Choral Symphony* is a famous example. As a rule, extended pieces are presented with deliberation. Instances such as the eighth symphony of Beethoven, which begins straight away with a fully-fledged and thoroughly organized theme, are comparatively rare.

ENDING

Problems of a different kind arise at the end of a piece. Our sense of form demands a reason why music, the phenomenon of sound which has been projected into time—whether for five minutes or an hour makes no basic difference—suddenly ceases. The feeling that the form has been completed is created by such means as the loosening and, finally, the disintegration of the structure; a definite final statement, or the dying away of the sound. The performer has to shape the music accordingly, and the slowing down of the tempo is only one of the means, and the most obvious, of bringing a piece to a halt. It cannot be often enough emphasized that the stereotyped exaggeration of *ritardandos* at the end is a bad mannerism. The fact that the music closes down should not be emphasized to a degree which distorts the features of the structure. Often a *ritardando* is composed and written out in broadening note-values, and often there are other features, such as a series of strong cadences, which make any additional *ritardando* superfluous, and therefore inadmissible. It is bad musical manners to stress what is made sufficiently plain by the notes.

## SHAPE

While it continues, music gains shape. We shall use the term *shape* for any group of notes that are felt as belonging together and make musical sense. A shape makes sense by virtue of its distinctive tonal and rhythmical features; and we comprehend it as a unit because we understand the relations and proportions of the features. A few examples will show how this is meant—how music begins to take shape.

*Haydn, String Quartet in C, Op. 76, No. 3, 2nd mvt.*

## MOTIF, PHRASE, CLAUSE

At the beginning of Haydn's old Austrian anthem we feel immediately that the first four notes, which cut across the bar line, belong together; they form a small rhythmic unit of the kind we call a *motif*. The motif is not yet a shape; distinctive features emerge only from the juxtaposition of the two motifs (a) and (a¹). It is by their different rhythms and melodic lines that the music gains shape and makes musical sense. The two motifs combine into the more developed unit of a *phrase*. The formal function of a motif is that of a germ from which larger forms develop. A phrase, on the other hand, consists of two or more, the same or different, motifs. A second phrase of two bars makes the structure grow into a unit of four bars, which we shall call a *clause*.[1] The motifs ($a^1$), ($a^2$) and ($a^3$) differ from motif (a), but the differences are not very great and their relations are obvious: motif ($a^1$) takes up the second half of (a), ($a^2$) is a variation of ($a^1$), and ($a^3$) resumes the trend upwards of (a). The relation of the motifs connects the two phrases, which are related and contrasted at the same time. So highly developed a melodic line, together with the harmony, makes for a closely knit structure.

Beethoven, Symphony No. 2 in D, Op. 36, 4th mvt.

The first two bars from the finale of Beethoven's second symphony show several distinct features. Though the first

[1] I am introducing the term *clause* for the combination of two (or more) phrases, because the term *sentence*, which is sometimes loosely applied, is also used, though with another significance (cf. pp. 95/96).

two notes are, in spite of their pointed rhythm, too insignificant to be taken for a shape, they are sufficiently defined to form a motif to be used later as a building stone. The first motif makes sense only in retrospect, by way of contrast to the second motif; and a shape emerges from this antithesis of juxtaposed motifs. Features of the second motif are: the sustained note C♯, which is intensified by a trill, and the subsequent leap from E to A on the full crotchet. Upbeats are characteristic of both motifs and, in a wider sense, the second motif may be regarded as an elaborate variation of the first. There are more features that link the two motifs: the notes G–C♯–E–A constitute the dominant seventh chord of the key; and the leap from the first motif's G to C♯ is reflected in the leap E–A. The harmonic structure is, therefore, based upon the dominant chord, whose notes are shared out between two distinct motifs. The *forte* dynamics and the unison of the orchestra are further features of the shape, which contrast sharply with the even quavers and the *piano* texture of the continuation.

*Verdi,* La Traviata, *Violetta's aria, 1st act*

The melody from Violetta's aria gains shape in descending a scale, but the interesting point is the scale's structure, which varies the motif (a), consisting of an *appoggiatura* and its resolution. *Appoggiaturas* impart the tension of dissonant notes to every beat; and the upbeat is vitalized by the passing note D♭, whose leap to the *appoggiatura* F delays the chief harmonic note E♭. The scale contains, by way of shortening the motif's values, four *appoggiaturas*, while the upbeat is an inversion of the motif. We see that the seemingly simple scale is a structure of some complexity, which should exclude an unduly speedy tempo—it would reduce the music's vitality, not increase it. The *pizzicato* arpeggios of the 'cello are an important feature of the accompaniment's texture and another hint that the quavers are to remain articulate.

The second phrase (B) takes up the *appoggiatura* motif, but now it goes to build a different structure. While the phrase (A) is highly integrated and closely knit, what follows is less elaborately shaped: the motif is not varied but merely repeated and this difference is of great consequence.

Variations of a motif provide formal links; repetitions, on the other hand, do not connect but set the repeated units side by side. Variation integrates, repetition groups. Variation makes the structure compact, repetition loosens it. In our example, the repetition of the motif in bars 3 and 4 provides a moment of relaxation after the tense descent of the scale and before the line turns upwards to form a shortened inversion of phrase (A). The second phrase ends as the first began. It is by virtue of their contrasting structures that together the two phrases form a higher, integrated unit—a *clause* of four bars.

Bach, The Well-Tempered Clavier, Book I, Fugue in C minor

In the theme of Bach's C minor fugue, motif (a) is rhythmically well-defined and developed, in that the mordent-like figure C–B–C is reflected by the following notes G–A♭. But it would be misleading to consider the particles of three and four notes as two motifs. Throughout the fugue the group of five notes forms a rhythmic unit. A shape emerges with the variation (a¹) of motif (a), whose D–G sharply contrasts to the former G–A♭. Together the two motifs form a phrase that comprises only one bar. The second phrase is an elaborate variation of both motifs (a¹) and (a); and the theme's main feature is the three different turns the motif takes: (b), (b¹), and (b²), a circumstance which easily encourages a wrong way of phrasing, based on the assumption that (a), (a¹) and (a²) are three phrases. It is important to group the theme into two phrases. While (b) and (b¹) form a distinct contrast, (b²) is similar to (b¹) and also resumes the progression G–A♭ of (b); thus (a²) is a résumé of (a) plus (a¹). If we were to play (a²) at the same level as (a) and (a¹), the note D of (b²) would be a weak echo of (b¹). No, there must be a slight respite of phrasing after (a¹), and (a²) must be begun afresh, aiming, not at the D but at the F.

*Mozart, Piano Quartet in G minor, K.478, 3rd mvt.*

In the finale of Mozart's piano quartet in G minor, we

have three motifs of contrasting rhythm and melodic design. The first (a) is essentially an elaboration of the note D, the chief features of the second (b) are the interval of a fifth and the syncopated rhythm. The juxtaposition of the two motifs seems to make sense but so far only part of the meaning has been revealed. The music continues with a sequential repetition of (b); and a third motif (c) concludes the phrase.

Harmony is an important component of the structure— it is fairly simple in our example, with the chords changing at every minim and the melody consisting chiefly of notes implied by the chords. However, the succession of five chords of the first inversion, the suspensions caused by the syncopations, and the two chromatic chords are significant harmonic features.

Two rhythmic features must influence the phrasing of the melody. The upbeat which opens the theme seems to demand an upbeat also for the second bar, but I believe that the last note D of the first bar still belongs to the first motif by way of phrasing it off; and that the second motif, in accordance with Mozart's slur, begins on the downbeat. Thus the first motif comprises five crotchets, and the second four—the extension of motif (a) is balanced by a contraction of the third (c). Nevertheless, it would be wrong distinctly to separate the second bar from the first. The last D, rather, should retain sufficient ambiguity to be felt as a possible upbeat. Features which are ambiguous, in that they fulfil two different, or even contradictory, functions, are often to be found in Mozart's structures. The second rhythmic feature is a consequence of the chromatic harmony of the third bar. The modulating sequential repetition of the second motif tends slightly to separate the third bar from the second—by way of a slight *rubato*—and to link it the closer to the fourth, a tendency strengthened by the fact that the bass remains the same.

The main theme from Debussy's *L'Après-midi d'un faune* is a not very developed, though highly characteristic,

77

*Debussy,* L'Après-midi d'un faune

structure. The note G (F double-sharp) is the pivot of the shape, and sustained notes give prominence to the tritone C♯–G. A moment of tension is the more acute as the G is only furtively introduced, by way of chromatic notes, and is really heard as F double-sharp. The subsequent diatonic introduction of A♮ is the second surprise—a surprise, which is as little spectacular as the other features of the melody and needs, if it is to be appreciated, a sense of subtle distinctions. The principal feature, melodic and harmonic at the same time, rests in the relation of C♯, as a latent pedal, to the antithesis which two groups of notes form, the first comprising A♯–(A♮)–G♯, the second, G–A. The rhythmical antithesis of a triplet and straight semiquavers is of secondary significance. But there is another feature of a different kind: throughout the piece the melody is entrusted to the flute, and its particular timbre, sweet and vague, is an essential component of the structure.

*Bach,* The Well-Tempered Clavier, *Book II, Fugue in A minor*

The theme of Bach's A minor fugue from the second volume of the *Forty-Eight* is throughout in disjunct motion. In the first phrase, motif (a) and its varied form (a¹) are juxtaposed, (a¹) assuming a wider leap than (a). The melodic

78

quality of the intervals and their harmonic implications are significant features of the structure; it is the diminished seventh, most prominent among them, which gives the phrase its character. Though the melodic shape of the first phrase is clearly defined, it is rhythmically uniform. The theme gains rhythmic distinction only with the second phrase, which is a diminution and at the same time an elaboration of the first.

*Wagner, Tristan und Isolde, 3rd act, sc. I, cor anglais solo*

The solo for the English horn from *Tristan* is without accompaniment. Its first phrase, of two bars, gains shape by juxtaposing a motif of two minims (a) and a shorter motif (b) which is immediately developed by imitating the rise of the first motif (b¹). While (a) expresses the key of F, only the second (b) makes the minor mode explicit by stressing D♭. In a second phrase, the short motif is further developed, and the clause ends with the minims of (a), but now in conjunct motion. The structure of the melody is highly organized melodically, harmonically (by implication) and rhythmically, though the rhythm is free of the ties of symmetry.

At the opening of Mozart's D minor quartet, the characteristic leap downwards that forms motif (a) is followed by a rhythmically elaborate second motif (b), which melodically inverts the descending octave and makes it a rising tenth. In fact, the second motif is derived from the first, in that its minim is split into repeated notes which are rhythmically defined, while the inverted leap of a tenth is delayed until the last quaver. The second motif gains momentum from the development of the harmony: the note D, at first

Mozart, String Quartet in D minor, K.421, 1st mvt.

representing the tonic, becomes in the second bar the major third of B♭ (the sixth degree of the key), a result of the progression of the bass. Whether the note F closes the first phrase of two bars, or acts as an upbeat to the next phrase, may seem doubtful. It is one of the structural ambiguities in which Mozart delights. The repetition of F on the full beat suggests an upbeat; the slur over the tenth interval, on the other hand (it is Mozart's own slur), indicates that D and F should be closely joined. Wide intervals need to be linked, or else they sound disconnected—as the term disjunct implies.

80

## TEXTURE

The texture of the accompaniment is an essential part of the structure. There are two strands in addition to the melody: the 'cello steps solemnly downwards and its minims give the harmony a new bass at every half bar; the off-beat quavers of the second violin and viola contrast rhythmically with the 'cello and complement the chords.

## ANTECEDENT, CONSEQUENT, PERIOD

After the disjunct intervals of the first phrase, the second is in conjunct motion and the four-bar clause ends on a half cadence. The four bars are repeated, but they close this time with a full cadence. We have a *rhythmic structure*, built symmetrically in that two similar clauses of equal length are juxtaposed. The rhythmic structure is a *period* of eight bars, whose two clauses are called respectively, *antecedent* and *consequent*. The consequent, however, is not an exact repetition of the antecedent. There is no identical repetition in music (or, for that matter, anywhere); every repetition is, in some way, a variation, for any second statement has a different weight and meaning from the first. In the case of the present period, the differences between antecedent and consequent are striking: the texture is lifted up to a higher octave, the dynamic is *f* instead of *p*, the 'cello joins in the off-beat rhythm, the harmony is varied, and finally there is a full cadence.

The opening two-bar phrase of the *Nocturne* by Chopin contains two motifs that are rhythmic contrasts, but melodically related. Both consist of a descending fourth, the first dragging on, the second compressed into quicker movement. The first begins before the bar, prematurely as it were, the second belatedly, after the beat. Or, rather, the second motif begins with the rests which replace the sustained note of the first. They do not interrupt the phrase, but add to its character of hesitation and weariness.

Chopin, Nocturne in G minor, Op. 37, No. I

The accompaniment helps to unite the two motifs. Its principal feature is the repeated progression E♭–D, which imitates in augmentation the *appoggiaturas* of the melody. An abundance of *appoggiaturas* intensifies the languid character of the music. But the character changes immediately with the second phrase: the line of the first is inverted, pacing up a sixth within one bar, though it took the whole of the first phrase to reach a similar interval in downward direction. Also, the texture of the accompaniment is more spacious than before. Together, the two contrasting phrases form the antecedent of a period.

Debussy's *Reflets dans l'eau* begins with a combination of three strands, of which the crotchet motif A♭–F–E♭ is not the principal part; alone, these notes would convey very little. The chief feature of the structure is the colour and line of the semiquaver chords, which rest on the pedal in the bass. A motif arises from the first three chords, and is repeated and telescoped. The rise and fall of the semiquavers is an antithesis—a 'reflection'—of the crotchets in the centre of the texture. And the balancing of the three strands, top, middle and bass, is the main task of the performer. They

Debussy, Images, 'Reflets dans l'eau'

Ex. 36

do not form a closely woven texture—the two upper strands, in semiquavers and crotchets respectively, seem freely and independently to float. But the similarity of their melodic lines gives an inkling of the piece's thorough organization.

### MUSIC GAINS SHAPE BY ANTITHESIS

Our examples, taken from various periods, styles and types of music, show how at the beginning of a piece two or more groups of notes are juxtaposed. The principle, though differently applied, remains the same: music gains shape by antithesis. Ever new relations and new shapes are created as the music continues. A shape may be short or long and may comprise any passage that is felt to be a unit, such as a phrase, clause, period, etc. We must take the expression 'shape' in its verbal sense, designating a limited, coherent entity. The cohesion may be close—if the shape comprises contrasting elements—or loose—if similar or only slightly varied motifs or phrases are combined. In this sense we speak of compact and loose structures. In general, diversity makes for compactness, uniformity for looseness. Repetition loosens, variation and contrast tighten the form. But loose and compact are only relative notions. The degrees of density change almost continuously. A loosely built phrase, followed by a compact one, may serve to connect the phrases more firmly by way of contrast. Harmony is one of the chief factors in structural density. In Haydn's melody (Ex. 26), it is largely the harmony that makes the structure firm; and in Ex. 30, we feel that the chromatic chord in bar 3 tightens the structure. Strong, cadential progressions make the form compact, sequences and modulations loosen it.

## THE STRUCTURAL ORGANIZATION OF SECTIONS

*Introductions*   The sections of which a piece consists are organized to accord with their different functions—as introductory or final, principal or secondary statements, transitions or episodes. Their structures show varying densities, the degree of which is dependent upon the shapes that are included. Introductions are loosely constructed and their shapes will scarcely be highly organized. Perhaps a single motif will be repeated without reaching a conclusion; or several motifs will line up without being closely connected. An introduction may even depict the notion of chaos, like the overture of Haydn's *Creation*.

*Principal Sections*   The shapes of principal sections will, as a rule, be highly organized, in that some of their melodic, rhythmic, harmonic or textural components will show, severally and combined, a number of distinctive features. Our previous examples give the openings of a few principal sections with significant melodic lines and motivic developments. In Exx. 30, 31, 32 and 34 the harmony plays an important part; in 34, 35 and 36, the texture is characteristic, in 31 and 36, the colour. The most highly organized shapes are those from the examples by Verdi (28), Mozart and Chopin; and the example from Debussy (36) shows that the looseness of the structure need not impair the degree of its organization.

*Subsidiary Sections*   In subsidiary sections, middle sections of ternary forms, for example, the shapes usually have fewer distinctive features, fewer motifs, less development and simpler harmony. But this must be taken with a grain of salt; sometimes the second subject of a sonata form is more highly organized than the first, especially if the principal subject is extended, and develops at a slow rate. In Mozart's *Jupiter* symphony and Schubert's *Unfinished*, the conciseness of the second subject contrasts with the diffuseness of the first.

*Transitions and Episodes*   Transitions are loosely shaped, often modulatory, and organized for the purpose of bridging more important sections. Episodes, on the other hand, have closely knit structures—they form more or less self-contained contrasts to surrounding passages.

*Closing Sections*   At the beginning, the music gains shape. At the end it loses shape, since the principles that consolidate the structure and make for its growth cease to be applied. Cadences, in particular, are apt to close a musical form, because they put a stop to the harmonic development by confirming the tonic. In short pieces the last cadence often coincides with the final development of the subject-matter, but in extended pieces there is always a point at which the melody ceases to carry the form and, even if maintained, becomes subject to harmony, viz., to cadence. The reappearance of the principal motif at the end of Mozart's E flat symphony, or the first movement of Beethoven's eighth symphony, makes very ingenious use of the cadence implied in the melody.

To recapitulate our findings: organization of the musical structure may embrace:

(*a*) the number of motifs, their relations and development;

(*b*) the direction, the intervals, and harmonic implications, of the melodic line;

(*c*) the number, length and grouping of rhythmic units;

(*d*) the pace at which the harmony develops, its complexity (degrees of richness, dissonances), its relation to a harmonic centre (tonality, cadence, modulation, modality, polytonality, composition with twelve notes);

(*e*) the texture (homophonic, polyphonic) and the tonal and rhythmic relations of its strands;

(*f*) the colour;

(*g*) dynamic differentiations.

The components of an organized structure are not developed equally. Structures complete in texture, such as fugues, will hardly allow for the elaborate variation of motifs that we meet in Mozart, for example; and a high degree of harmonic organization will make for simpler features in other ways (cf. Ex. 52, p. 105). Over-organization would cloud the structure. The sections of the form are differentiated not only by different features, but also by different methods of organization.

## VARIATION, REPETITION, CONTRAST

We have seen that the features of a shape include some that are alike and some that are different. Every antithesis contains similar and diverse elements. Variation is the basic principle of musical organization, a principle which makes at the same time for diversity and for unity of form.[1] Features of melody and rhythm are continually subjected to variation; in harmonic variation it is chords that change; variation of the texture alters the melody's accompaniment or the number of polyphonic strands; and variation of colour is provided by differentiated scoring. A change of dynamics, on the other hand, will be felt as contrast rather than as variation. *Variations on a theme*, as a category of musical form, is a special case; a sequence of short pieces is derived from a model by way of changed structural features.

The principle of variation implies two complementary principles: repetition and contrast. Any motif, phrase, clause

[1] 'Variation is that kind of repetition which changes some of the features of a unit, motif, phrase, segment, section, or larger part, but preserves others. To change everything would prevent there being any repetition at all, and thus might cause incoherence.' (Schoenberg, *Models for Beginners in Composition*.)

or larger form may be repeated, varied, or contrasted with another. The three principles are akin, for every repeat is in some way a variation, and every contrast must preserve the context. It depends upon the quality and quantity of the changed features whether a passage is felt as a repetition or a contrast; or whether it is a variation in a narrower sense.

Chopin, Prelude No. 7 in A, Op. 24

In Ex. 37, the motif of two bars is varied three times, but in spite of melodic and harmonic changes, the variations of the motif are less strongly felt than its rhythmic uniformity.

The first and second subjects of Schubert's sonata in D major (the second subject is quoted as it appears in the recapitulation) have melodic outlines in common, though the first is in conjunct, the second in disjunct motion. Both rise to the dominant and fall back to the tonic; and in both the dominant is reached by way of the sixth: B♭–G–A in the principal theme, B♮–G♯–A in the second. The change of rhythmic, melodic and textural features, however, obscures what they have in common and makes the second theme a contrast to the first. Nevertheless, the relation can still be felt.

*Schubert, Piano Sonata in D, Op. 53, 1st mvt. (1st subject)*

Allegro vivace

*Schubert, Piano Sonata in D, Op. 53, 1st mvt. (2nd subject)*

Allegro vivace

Variation of a prominent feature naturally causes greater structural changes than variation of a subordinate feature. Since rhythm is the most conspicuous element, its presentation will maintain the connection between other, heterogeneous features. But if the rhythm is altered, the outlook becomes very different.

The third bar of Ex. 40 paraphrases the note A of the first; though everything else is unchanged, the different rhythm stands out. It need not be emphasized by the performer. On the contrary, if he modifies the expression he will play the figure of the third bar more softly, in order to assimilate it

Schubert, Piano Sonata in A, Op. posth., 2nd mvt.

Andantino

Ex.40

into the sound of the sustained notes. Five notes are louder than one—at least on the piano. The melody of the Chopin *Prelude*, on the other hand (cf. Ex. 37), needs subtle emphasis of the motif's variations by varied dynamics, colours and *rubatos*.

Our examples overleaf from the *Fantastic Symphony* of Berlioz give the principal theme (the *idée fixe*, as Berlioz calls it) of the first movement (A), and some of its transformations in the later movements (B–D). We have here an instance of rhythmic variation, while the line of the melody remains unchanged. The intervals of the theme are sufficiently significant to be remembered, and when they appear in different guises, the new shapes are recognized as variations, each of which represents a different character.

Repetitions of motifs or phrases tend to keep the structure loose and open; they are constructive in so far as they effect a certain symmetrical order. Symmetry co-ordinates, but does not integrate. It is the subsequent elements of contrast which, in retrospect, link parallel shapes.

### MOTIVIC STRUCTURE

At the beginning of Mozart's G minor symphony (cf. Ex. 42) the music gains shape, not with the repetitions of the *appoggiatura* motif, but with the rise of a sixth. The repeated motifs do not refer to each other, but to the common goal of the interval of a sixth, which brings relief. A moment of expectation is created by the exact repetitions

*Berlioz, Fantastic Symphony, Op. 14*

   *A: 1st mvt.* Rêveries: Passions
   *B: 2nd mvt.* Valse
   *C: 3rd mvt.* Scène aux champs
   *D: 5th mvt.* Songe d'une nuit du Sabat

of the motif, and the note D from which the line surges upwards, is the melodic centre of the phrase. The crotchets D–B♮ do not add up to a new motif, but are a variation—an extension—of the first. While the tension grows, the quavers of the *appoggiaturas* broaden imperceptibly—the minute broadening (*rubato obbligato*) is a function of the structure.

## THE MELODIC STRUCTURE

The structure of the first four-bar clause is by no means as regular as it appears to be when reading the music. Rhythmically the two phrases (A) and (B) are symmetrical, but their melodic structures are very different, antithetical, in fact—and there can be no doubt that melodic elements are the principal features of the theme. The conjunct descent from B♭ to C corresponds more closely to the disjunct rise D–B♭ than to the initial repetitions of the *appoggiatura* motif; the descent is an antithesis to the climactic rise. While the first phrase (A) grows, the second (B) relaxes. And the two crotchets C on which (B) comes to rest are less significant than the earlier crotchets of the sixth; they are a counterpart of the first motif. According to customary motivic analysis, the scheme of the four-bar clause is ABBA, but this is an interpretation which contradicts the melodic facts. Our structural analysis yields ABBA—a scheme which agrees with the performer's approach.

## THE RHYTHMIC STRUCTURE

The structure of the theme shows many distinct features, such as the strangely short opening solo of the accompanying violas, anticipating the sixth and omitting the fifth of the minor triad—the entry of the theme thus oscillates between a major and a minor chord. We shall have to return to this interesting structure on later occasions. But let us consider for a moment the rhythmic structure of the whole theme of nineteen (or with the opening, twenty) bars. It is what we call a *sentence*. The first clause of four bars is sequentially repeated on another degree, and followed by shorter shapes, most of them derived from the first. The sequence (X) com-

prises twice four bars; a repeated phrase (Y) twice two bars; and a cadence (Z), which leads to the dominant, stressed by further cadences: three of one bar and two of half a bar. During the last cadences the rhythm of the *appoggiatura* motif appears three times[1] in the bass—echoed later by the re-entry of the theme. The groups of different lengths form a loose chain which is fastened by cadences.

## SENTENCE

The overall shape of a sentence is loose. This will become evident if we compare a sentence (43) with another, more compact form (44).

*Beethoven, Piano Sonata in F minor, Op. 2, No. 1, 1st mvt.*

---

[1] In fact, it appears twice three times (though in all only five times). The last of the first three repeats is also the first of the second three repeats. Musical arithmetic often counts things twice, the last event of the past being also the first of events to come.

Mozart, Symphony No. 40 in G minor, K.550, 4th mvt.

The theme of Beethoven's F minor sonata is a sentence, that of the finale from Mozart's G minor symphony a simple ternary form. Both examples have the first phrase in common, which in the sentence goes to form a *sequence* by way

94

of free repetitions, but in the larger form is followed by a sharply contrasting second phrase. This antithesis joins the shapes of two phrases into the longer shape of a four-bar clause. In the sentence, sequences keep the form loose, especially when the phrase is reduced to motif (b), which is again repeated; thus the rhythmic units of the eight-bar sentence grow shorter (twice two bars and twice one bar), until a cadence to the dominant (of two bars) temporarily provides a halt. The first half of the ternary form, on the other hand, is completed by a sequential repetition of the complete four-bar clause. In this instance, the sequence does not loosen the form, but balances its two halves—the antithesis has made the structure sufficiently compact. Harmonic features, especially cadences and the distribution of tonic and dominant, help to loosen and secure the shapes of both structures.

In the middle section of the present ternary form, two contrasting motifs, (c) and (d), go to form a shape whose exact repetition keeps the structure loose; but the last four bars resume the second clause of the first section, and thus firmly interlink the structure of the ternary form. Unlike immediate repetition, the later resumption of earlier features consolidates the form.

## THE PERIOD

A clear distinction should be made between a sentence and a period—there is much confusion in the use of the terms. In a *sentence*, the first phrase or clause is immediately repeated—more or less exactly and often in the form of a sequence—and developed further by way of variations, in the course of which the phrase (or clause) is reduced to shorter rhythmic units. In a *period*, the second phrase is an antithesis to the first, and both together form a larger rhythmic unit (the antecedent). Antecedent and consequent show similar features, and are sometimes almost identical; they are built in a symmetrical relation and make the period

95

a well-balanced and compact form. The antecedent ends usually on a half close, the consequent on a full close.

Periods are sometimes very highly organized. The Andante from Mozart's *Kleine Nachtmusik* may serve as an example. The two phrases of the antecedent consist of four

Mozart, Serenade, Eine kleine Nachtmusik, K.525, 2nd mvt.

different motifs which, however, are related to each other. The chief feature of motif (a) is the quaver E repeated between quaver rests; on the corresponding beats of (b) there are repeated F's, while the rests are replaced by notes that play in thirds around F and G; motif (c) shortens the value of the repeated notes by way of syncopation; (d) varies (c); and with (b¹) the antecedent turns to the dominant. The consequent resumes the first phrase, but the second phrase is further varied, and the full cadence to the tonic is harmonically and melodically enriched.

Rhythmic and melodic diversity increase the consistency of a form. The structure of the well-known melody from Haydn's *Clock* symphony is a fine example of superior melodic and rhythmic organization. In the first phrase, motifs in disjunct and conjunct motion, (a) and (b), are juxtaposed. The conjunct descent from B to D mirrors the disjunct rise B–G. The rhythmic uniformity of the second phrase contrasts with the diversity of the first. The melody

*Haydn, Symphony No. 101 in D (The Clock), 2nd mvt.*

Ex.46

is a period of nine bars, whose consequent is prolonged by an inserted variation of motif (b).

Periods are essentially symmetrical structures, but need not be grouped in units of two, four, eight, etc., bars. The following example from the Minuet of Haydn's string quartet, Op. 54, No. 1, shows a period of ten bars, whose antecedent and consequent comprise five bars each.

*Haydn, String Quartet in G, Op. 54, No. I, 3rd mvt.*

The phrasing of this period calls for a longer 'mental breath' than the customary periods of eight bars.

Ex. 48 is a sentence of fourteen bars, where a three-bar phrase is twice repeated before it is reduced to briefer shapes.

### EXTENSION AND CONTRACTION

Sometimes, the squareness of symmetry is broken by the extension of one rhythmic unit which is then balanced by the contraction of another; or, *vice versa*, a contraction is

*Mozart, Symphony No. 40 in G minor, K.550, 3rd mvt.*

balanced by an extension. In the Andante of the *Clock* symphony (cf. Ex. 46), it is the solitary bar of introduction which is the cause of the consequent's extension. The single bar is felt to be part of the antecedent's rhythmic structure, which thus consists of three-plus-two bars, answered in the consequent by two-plus-three bars.

The main theme of Schubert's 'great' C major symphony combines contraction and expansion. Two phrases, one of two bars, the other of only one bar, go to form a clause of three bars. The second phrase is a reduction of the first, and, though consisting of a single motif, gains its own distinct shape on the strength of its melodic contrast to

99

*Schubert, Symphony No. 7 in C, Op. posth., 1st mvt.*

motif (b). The weight of the short phrase is clearly felt, especially when, after a varied repetition of the three-bar clause, the augmentation of (b¹) serves to extend the rhythmic structure. The theme thus consists of eight bars, grouped into three phrases ($2 \times 3$ bars and $1 \times 2$ bars). It goes without saying that the performer has to observe the niceties of rhythmic groupings by graded commas; wrong phrasing distorts the structure.

The significance of repetition and symmetry varies with the style of the music. In Stravinsky's ballet *Orpheus*, there is a beautiful, highly organized melody, whose first section forms a period of eighteen bars. It is Orpheus's *Air de Danse*, which 'soothes the tormented souls of Tartarus'. The changes of time signature do not obscure the rhythmic structure. They should be felt as *rubatos*, which have not been left to the discretion of the performer, but composed. The antecedent contains three phrases; the first of two bars ($3/8+2/8$) and the second of three ($3/8+2 \times 2/8$) are juxtaposed in antithesis. The third phrase, of four bars, is more loosely shaped. It begins with an upbeat, develops motif (f), and closes with motif (c) on the tonic. The consequent comprises nine bars, like the antecedent, and is similarly built, but the cadence turns to the dominant, C.

In Schoenberg's works almost every repetition amounts to a variation; and shapes are regarded as similar which in a different context might appear only remotely related. The

Stravinsky, Orpheus, 'Air de Danse'

theme of the Variations from his *Serenade*, Op. 24, is a
period of eleven bars (51).

Antecedent and consequent consist of the same notes and
motifs, but the consequent exposes the notes in retrograde
motion, and the motifs appear on different beats. The antecedent, of five bars, contains four motifs; the consequent,
of five-and-a-half bars, omits motif (c) but adds a cadence:
A–B♭ (extension).

*Schoenberg, Serenade, Op. 24, 3rd mvt.*

## DISTINCTIONS OF MUSICAL STRUCTURES— THE STRUCTURAL DENSITY

Shapes, of course, can be grouped in countless ways, and the rhythmic structures that result are too many and too varied for classification. Even comparatively simple forms, such as periods or sentences cannot be defined exactly. There are periods which contain elements of a sentence, and *vice versa*. But we can perhaps find a few principles for the performer's guidance.

A rhythmic structure consists of at least two phrases, and may be a clause, period, sentence, or any integrated, composite unit. The number of shapes unfolded in the unit and the degree of their relationship are of paramount importance for the style of the music and its performance. Structures rich in details need clear presentation, but it is wrong to over-stress points which the composer makes explicit himself.

The rate at which the structure grows by development of motifs and shapes—the structural density—must dictate the performer's approach. Closely knit structures should not be unduly overburdened with details, but elucidated by clarity of delivery. Nor should loosely built structures be tightened by too elaborate an interpretation.

Repetitions of motifs or phrases should never be automatic; the performer must be aware of their meaning within the context. They do not always loosen the form. At the beginning of a piece or section, a repeated motif may create a moment of tension; in the middle of a rhythmic structure, a repeated unit may resume a point made earlier, and in this way form a link.

A rhythmic structure may be open or closed, i.e., self-contained and balanced, or unbalanced and demanding a continuation. There are pieces that end with an open structure, with a query, as it were.

Harmony often supports rhythmic structures by emphasizing their features. Cadences of graded definition clarify the grouping of phrases, clauses, etc.; the delay effected by an interrupted cadence may coincide with a rhythmic extension. And it is largely the harmony that makes for an open, or a closed, structure.

Symmetry, is not, of course, an indispensable feature of rhythmic structures. Schoenberg compared rhythmic symmetry to poetic verse. But musical prose exists too, in old and new music, and not only in recitative. Fugue is an essentially non-symmetrical form. Phrases of different length in homophonic music can also yield balanced rhythmic forms, the English horn melody from *Tristan*, for instance, whose opening is shown in Ex. 33.

## MELODIC STRUCTURES

Rhythm, because it groups the notes, is the chief organizing factor in music. It is this rhythmic grouping of the notes which makes the melody comprehensible. A melody's two components, line and rhythm, are not always of equal importance. There are melodies in which the rhythmic element prevails, as in dances and similar pieces; and there are melodies of *cantabile* character, e.g., Ex. 26, in which the melodic design is the dominant feature. The per-

103

former should know whether a melody is of the rhythmic or *cantabile* type.

Organization of melodic design is based on the relations of intervals. We feel that such relations have definite qualities. Each interval has its own distinct character, though some notes have closer affinities than others. Further relationships are established by the particular order in which the notes are arranged. A melodic structure is defined by the relations of the notes, both to each other and to a tonal (in the wide sense of the word) system, be the system the major, the minor, a church mode, the pentatonic scale or a note-row.[1]

The variations of motifs, by which musical structures grow, usually involve more changes of intervals than of rhythm. A rhythmic change is a radical departure from the original shape (cf. pp. 86–89). Among structural features it is, as a rule, the melodic line that shows, relatively, the greatest variety.[2]

The relations of the melodic line to a tonal system have harmonic significance.

## HARMONIC STRUCTURES

The role of harmony within the structure has changed during the musical ages. In most works of the eighteenth and nineteenth centuries harmony is as important as, and sometimes more prominent than, melody and rhythm.

---

[1] The established system, i.e., the way the notes are grouped, tends to colour the intrinsic character of the intervals in a peculiar way. In the minor, for instance, the diminished seventh sounds different from the major sixth, though both, at least in the accepted system of equal temperament, are the same interval.

[2] Rhythmic variation of a note-row is a permanent feature of composition with twelve notes, and of serial techniques in key-centred music. But a similar method of maintaining the melodic outlines while the rhythm changes is often found in older music. The contrasting themes of Schubert's D major Sonata (cf. Exx. 38 and 39) are connected in this way.

Wagner, Siegfried, *1st act, Wanderer Motive*

Moderato

Ex.52

In our example, the *Wanderer* theme from Wagner's *Siegfried*, the burden of the structure rests on the harmony. The melodic design is not very significant; the rhythmic structure consists of two sequences, each of three times two bars, whose squareness is interrupted by a modulating extension after the first sequence; the harmonic structure, however, is highly organized and yields a rich four-part texture. Sequences repeat the melody, but vary the harmony by transposition to other degrees. The sequence seems to modulate to D minor, E minor, F major, B♭ major, A minor, E minor, and A minor in succession. But the key is A minor—though most of the chords are chromatic and the tonic is never in the root position. The chromatic chords

105

are secondary dominants, which lead to, or stand for, degrees of the key, viz., the subdominant, minor dominant, submediant, and Neapolitan sixth. The very first chord is a secondary dominant (on the tonic) of the key's subdominant. The theme is an example of what Schoenberg calls *extended tonality*.

Highly organized harmonic structures of a very different kind abound among Bach's harmonizations of old German hymn tunes. The tune of the chorale from the *St. John*

**Bach, St. John Passion,** *Chorale,* '*Wer hat dich so geschlagen*'

*Passion* is a period of twelve bars. The antecedent ends on a
half close, the consequent on a perfect cadence, otherwise
both are identical and consist of three phrases whose melodic
lines are neatly contrasted. Bach's arrangement not only
makes the consequent a harmonic variation of the antecedent, but illuminates every note so that the melodic design
stands out, as in relief. The ends of the phrases are stressed
by elaborate cadences which make use of secondary dominants; the first comes to rest on the dominant of the submediant, the second on the mediant, the third and fifth on
the dominant, and the fourth on the dominant of the supertonic.

## HARMONIC VARIATION

The principle of variation is widely applied in harmonic
structures. The harmonic functions of one chord may be
assumed by another, if it is a suitable substitute. For
example, the root position of a chord may be replaced by an
inversion, the dominant by a diminished seventh chord, the
supertonic or the subdominant by a Neapolitan sixth. A
melody may be given various harmonic interpretations as
in the antecedent and consequent of Bach's chorale. If the
performer is not aware of the harmonic relations within a
structure, he is bound to make mistakes.[1] Let us take
another example from the G minor symphony of Mozart,
this time from the Andante (54).

The sudden change of dynamics and texture in the eighth
bar is so surprising that some conductors consider the *forte*
passage a contrasting episode, to be distinguished from the
preceding melody by heavier movement or even a slower
tempo. But the passage is part of the second subject, a
rhythmic structure that should not be split. The melody is
a period whose consequent begins as a textural variation of
the antecedent, and in the eighth bar there is a harmonic
variation: the subdominant turns into the minor. In four

[1] The place of harmony within musical form is described in great
detail in Schoenberg's book *Structural Functions of Harmony*.

*Mozart, Symphony No. 40 in G minor, 2nd mvt.*

Andante

bars of elaborate cadence, Mozart returns to, and at the same time confirms, the tonic (which is here temporarily, at the end of the exposition, B flat). The *forte* passage is an extension of the period, balanced by an unusually short codetta. It is not to be treated as a separate entity; in fact, the movement should go ahead and stress the melody's continuity. We may note among the features of the minor passage that the quaver rhythm is derived from the first theme, which itself also anticipates the minor subdominant by way of G♭ in the bass. The minor region has previously been stressed by the modulations of the bridge passage; and *p-f* contrasts have also occurred earlier on. The surprise, we see, is well prepared.

In a sense, a subdominant is likely to widen the scope of the key. The dominant tends towards the tonic; the tonic, in turn, has a similar relation to the subdominant and can be made to function as its dominant. With the tonic as centre, the tendency of the subdominant is centrifugal, while that of the dominant is centripetal. A cadence, in which the tonic is preceded by both subdominant and dominant, balances the two opposing tendencies. In Ex. 30, the subdominant of the second bar marks a departure from the tonic which is counteracted by the subsequent chromatic chords. And the sweep of the *Wanderer* theme (cf. Ex. 52) is largely due to its departure from the subdominant.

### THE RATE OF HARMONIC PROGRESSION

The rate at which the harmony proceeds is an important feature of a structure and of special significance for its rhythmic content. Chords usually do not change with every note of the melody, but progress mostly in a different rhythm. The accompaniment of Ex. 46 shows a change of harmony only in the fourth bar, a late harmonic development which, however, sets the melody delightfully into relief by stressing at the same time the change in its rhythmic structure. The first two bars form, and are to be phrased as, a single rhythmic unit, but in the third bar each quaver needs a light accent. In general, slow development of the harmony with few chordal changes makes for extended shapes, or broad exposition of the music, while concentrated harmonic progressions are likely to tighten the structure or bring it to a close. Cadences, in fact, usually show an increase of melodic and rhythmic density. Other features may, of course, counter the pace of the harmonic change and make for broad exposition of the structure in spite of a richly developed harmony. The sequences of the *Tristan* Prelude (cf. Ex. 73, Chapter IV, p. 144) are a case in point. The rate of harmonic progression is a factor of which the performer must take account, especially when he determines the tempo of a piece. In some of Bach's preludes, for instance, melodic patterns and slow, regular changes of the harmony are almost the only significant features of the structure (cf. Chapter II, p. 31, Ex. 5). The chief task of the performer is to realize the character of the figurations and yet choose a tempo that preserves the continuity of the slowly changing chords; if the tempo is too slow the harmonic scheme is broken—over-stretched.

## HARMONY VERSUS MELODY

As a rule, chordal accompaniments realize the harmony implied by the melody, but not every melody is unequivocally based on a particular harmony, or on any harmony whatsoever. There are melodies whose harmony is made explicit by their structure, but others, as those of chorales, which permit various harmonic interpretations. The chords of an accompaniment do not register every turn the melody is taking, yet *appoggiaturas*, suspensions and passing notes are not without harmonic significance. On the contrary, the dissonances that they form enliven the harmony. In his harmonization of a Hungarian peasant song, Bartók uses chords which are certainly not implied by the melody; they do not blend with it, but heighten its effect. Here, in respect of both rhythm and melody, the song and its accompaniment are two strands which form a kind of duet; and as such the music should be played.

A modulation can be expressed in a single melodic line. In the last act of Bizet's opera *Carmen*, there is, within a

Bartók, 15 Hungarian Peasant Songs for Pianoforte, No. 1

Ex. 55

passage in E flat major (56), a model middle section which returns to the original key in a very direct and convincing way. The first note of the modulating bar is felt, in retrospect, as a chromatic E♮, which together with the subsequent G forms a kind of double *appoggiatura* before the fifth (F) of the dominant (B♭). A slight *rubato* (cédez) on the last notes F–G is obviously required (cf. bars 11–12).

## TEXTURE

Harmonic relations must be sized up and realized by the performer according to the merits of each case. He should always keep in mind that chords, as well as homophonic and polyphonic textures, serve the purpose of enriching the

Bizet, Carmen, *4th act*

Moderato

sound, not of making it louder. Textures whose strands represent more than one key should be similarly assessed. Bitonality is a kind of extended tonality. A beautiful example of triple tonality occurs in Benjamin Britten's opera, *The Turn of the Screw*.

Britten, The Turn of the Screw, 2nd act, sc. 3

Ex. 57

Three strands, a melody in F major, the bass in F minor, and an accompaniment in B flat minor, form a tense *forte* texture, whose clashing false relations serve a particular dramatic purpose; they express the courage of a woman who is not by nature heroic.

## BALANCE OF THE TEXTURE

The distinction between homophonic and polyphonic music is less important for the performer than for the historian. In a sense, every texture is polyphonic, and the features of each strand must be taken into account. In homophonic music, harmonic relations are supposed to be of greater significance than in polyphonic, but harmony is only one of the structural components. Melodic and rhythmic features are, as a rule, more important, even when the strand may form only an accompaniment. Even Albertibasses should, I think, be phrased individually, if discreetly —otherwise they do not 'sound'. For the performer, the chief textural problem is balancing the notes. If he is a pianist, the balance is literally in his own hands. He can colour a chord by giving its constituent notes different weights. The top is the first fiddle of a piano texture, but need not always be played louder than the other strands. By giving prominence to an inner part of the texture, say for the sake of clarifying a modulation, the colour changes at the same time. Independent fingers can add much variety to the tone of the piano; the bass needs as much attention as the treble, because the clarity of texture depends upon its precision.

In chamber music, balance of the texture is, of course, team work. In contributing his share, each member should realize the individual character of his part. Often, players try to adapt and blend their *timbres*, thus matching the tone of their instruments. But it makes for cleaner and more colourful textures if the *timbres* remain differentiated— balance can be obtained by carefully adapted dynamics. String quartets, in particular, should differentiate their *timbres* more boldly than is their custom. When the players meet in a chord or chordal passage, I often feel embarrassed by a sudden thickening of the tone through reinforced resonances, which are, no doubt, a consequence of mutually adjusted *timbres*.

Conditions are different with the motley *timbres* of the orchestra. In order to achieve adequate balance, the individual *timbres* must often be adjusted, especially if the score lacks the neutralizing effect of woodwind in triplicate. It is the different dynamic range of the instruments as well as their disparate *timbres* that can easily upset the balance of sound. Merely to level dynamics does not suffice. Without a proper balance of *timbres*, many *forte* passages sound muddled, especially *tutti* passages of classical concertos which, after a soloist's refined playing, burst in the more irritatingly.

Rhythmic balance is another problem. The various instruments do not produce the notes with equal ease, and do not respond to the conductor's beat at an equal rate. Good orchestral musicians take this fact into account, and good conductors are capable of obtaining precise ensemble playing. Precision lies not only in beginning but also in ending the notes exactly together. It makes for a muddy sound if some of the players sustain the notes longer or with fuller tone than the others, especially at the end of a phrase. On the other hand, precision is a musical virtue that should be practised with discretion. Sensitive phrasing is often at cross-purposes with the note-values, and the melody need not exactly coincide in every semiquaver with the rest of the texture. What Mozart wrote about the independence of the hands in a *rubato*, should make us think. Exaggerated precision sometimes hampers the phrasing and obliterates the colour.

Balancing the *timbres* of the orchestra is an art that not all conductors understand. Luckily, the musicianship of

*Beethoven, Symphony No. 3 in E flat (Eroica), Op. 55, 1st mvt.*

orchestral players helps to shape such well-known but delicate passages as the bridge section in the first movement of the *Eroica* (58).

A one-bar motif is alternatingly played by different instruments and goes to form a structure of twelve bars, grouped into three four-bar phrases. The different *timbres* serve to loosen the structure—the passage is transitional—but subtle colouring must sufficiently adjust the *timbres* to each other in order to preserve the continuity of each phrase. To be always listening to his colleagues, and to adapt his performance accordingly, should be a matter of course among musicians. It is a question not only of dynamics and phrasing, but also of colouring the *timbres*.

## COLOUR AS A STRUCTURAL FEATURE

There are instances in which melodic, rhythmic and other features recede, and colour emerges as the principal factor of the structure. Chords are not only constructive as components of harmony, but also contribute a large share

Mozart, String Quartet in C, K.465, 1st mvt.

to what is felt as colour. In general, dissonances are more colourful than consonances: the ear, not immediately aware of their harmonic implications, takes them at their face value, i.e., as aural sensations. We need not look to modern music for examples.

The introduction to Mozart's *Dissonance* quartet leaves the key in abeyance for quite a while, nor does melody or rhythm gain defined shape; and the sequence formed from the first bars leads us only further astray. The structure is loose and open, and its principal feature is the colour of the widely spaced four-part texture.

The 'sleep motif' from Wagner's *Siegfried* (cf. Ex. 9, p. 36) consists chiefly of a chain of common chords, whose lack of apparent harmonic relationship heightens their colouristic affect. False relations abound, and yet they sound fascinatingly smooth, not least because the scoring absorbs the *timbres* (triple woodwind!) and makes for an organ-like, velvety texture.

Colour gains structural eminence in Debussy's music; the other features serve to enhance its variety. His melodies are short phrases, his harmony avoids cadences and any development that tightens the form. He indulges in the softest dynamics, but his transparent textures are highly organized. Exact repetitions of short but complex structures convey the impression of a music that is static rather than moving forward. Visual associations are evoked, not only by suggestive titles. Adequate performance of Debussy's music depends on a sympathetic understanding of his half-shades and twilights.

In the seventh piece of the second volume of Preludes (*La terrasse des audiences du clair de lune*), the pianist would be absolutely wrong if he stressed the top notes of the chords; the four-part texture of the chords must be well balanced and each note equally distinct. Neither the melody nor the harmony is very significant in itself, but only as a component part of a complex structure, whose chief feature lies in the colour of the texture. The harmony rests on the

Debussy: Preludes *for Pianoforte, Book II, 'La Terrasse de saudiences du clair de lune'*

dominant by way of a pedal. Clearly, any harmonic implications of the chord-clusters are less important than their colouristic quality.

The 'emancipation of the dissonance' (cf. Chapter II/1,

p. 33) has greatly increased music's colouristic capacity. In Schoenberg's piano pieces, Op. 11, the harmony is not subject to a key. A two-bar phrase, taken from the second piece, shows very bright colours, a consequence of dissonant chords.

*Schoenberg, Piano Piece, Op. 11, No. 2*

A succession of three-part chords forms the introduction to the fourth piece from *Pierrot lunaire* ('Eine blasse Wäscherin').

*Schoenberg, Pierrot lunaire, Op. 21, 4th piece, 'Eine blasse Wäscherin'*

By varying the distribution of the notes, Schoenberg creates continually changing colours. The flute, for example, plays the bottom part of the first chord, the top of the second, and the middle part of the third. Clearly, a change of colour would not succeed if the players were to adjust their colours instead of maintaining their natural *timbres*. Equal dynamics and rhythmic precision are indispensable requirements for balancing the disparate sounds, but a rigorously strict tempo must be avoided.

## VOCAL AND INSTRUMENTAL MUSIC

The same principles of form are shared alike by instrumental and vocal music, but the conditions of performance are very different. The singer is himself the instrument on which he performs. Among music's principal soloists, the singer tires more quickly than the pianist or violinist, and his exertions affect not only the tone production but the instrument itself. Vocal solo pieces are therefore less developed and, in consequence, shorter than instrumental ones. The singer's concertos are arias or cantatas.

The singer's words are, musically considered, an element of colour; the vowels contribute a variety of *timbres*, while the consonants are percussive—the continuants with fixed pitch, the explosives without pitch. But the words charge the music with the meaning they express, and this fact is of great consequence for the musical form. In order not to overburden and thus obscure the structure, vocal melodies are, in general, of a simpler type than instrumental ones. If the words are meant to be understood, the degree of structural complexity has to be limited. The *tessitura* and dynamic range of a normal voice are comparatively narrow; nevertheless, the singer must compete with his instrumental colleagues not by clinging to the meaning of the words, but by shaping the music. Apart from the direct appeal of the human voice, he has the advantage of the rich colouristic resources that vowels and consonants supply. Words are to be treated as a component of the musical structure.

The voice is a melodic instrument, and the singer is less at ease with short notes and fast rhythms. Consonants help to articulate the notes, but must be projected so rapidly that even at the quickest speed the vowels have sufficient time to ring out.

Voices and instruments are different agencies of sound. Rarely treated on an equal footing, they go to form a two-fold structure where the vocal part is prominent. In song, the voice delivers the gist of the message which the accompaniment complements, supports, colours or elaborates. The music is on two planes, one of which is a foil to the other; both accompanist and singer should unite in enhancing each other's parts. In this respect, the task of the singer is the easier, because the accompaniment helps him to find the mood and character of the piece; he must be aware of the features, such as motifs, or rhythms, of particular relevance to his own melody, especially those that occur in *ritornellos* and interludes; and he should not close so slowly that the accompanist's postlude or final cadences cease to make sense.

Accompanying is a question not only of musicianship, but also of tact. It goes without saying that the accompanist must understand the structure of the singer's part as well as the structure of his own. If there are differences of opinion, the decision of the singer, as the more responsible artist, must prevail—though singers are sometimes accessible to reasoned argument! On the other hand, the accompanist should not distort his part by suddenly yielding to every *rubato* of the singer, but shape the music so that the singer's *rubatos* coincide with his own. His principal task is to balance colour and dynamics. In this instance, adjustment of the textures is often necessary, though a certain degree of differentiation is required if the accompaniment is elaborate.

The parts of voice and accompaniment are not organized in the same way. While the voice carries the melody together with the words, the accompaniment is responsible for the form as a whole. It begins, as a rule, earlier, and closes later than the voice, thus providing a second ending. *Ritornellos* are short; they are preludes and interludes which anticipate either the melody of the song or its character. In Violetta's aria from *La Traviata* (cf. Ex. 28), immediately before our example begins, an orchestral *ritornello* anticipates the melody but breaks off in the seventh bar. Schubert's *ritornellos* often contribute points of interest to the musical interpretation of the words by introducing phrases which differ from the melody in the voice. Sometimes the singer's part is included in the accompanying texture, but more often the two structures are melodically and rhythmically dissimilar; such features as they have in common go to form different shapes. A similar two-fold structure prevails in any type of accompanied vocal works, including oratorios and operas.

## STRUCTURE AND CHARACTER

It will, by now, have become evident in what sense the character of the music is expressed through the structure; and why it should be a performer's paramount concern to take the structural features of a work into account. There is no other means of access to correct performance than by way of the music's structure. Rightly understood, it reveals the phrasing and tempo that are required for clearly projecting every detail. Often, some of the features are immediately obvious, but it is the most conspicuous features that need not always be emphasized in performance. In Ex. 29, the repeated figure C–B–C is an obvious feature of the fugal theme, but the three different turns of motif (a) require the performer's careful attention. To judge the relative importance of structural features is not always easy. When this is so, opinions inevitably vary and may present a legitimate cause for different interpretations.

The course which a performer's deliberations may take

will be seen from the structural analysis of a well-known piece, Schumann's *Träumerei*. Its first four-bar clause serves as an example.

*Schumann, Kinderszenen, Op. 15, 'Träumerei'*

Ex.63

A few distinctive features are immediately apparent: Motif (a) moves from a crotchet upbeat to a sustained strong beat, and consists, melodically, of the dominant C leaping a fourth upwards to the tonic F. The motif is extremely simple, but we shall see what it has in store for us. The sustained tonic chord on the second beat is a significant textural feature. Together with the bass on the first beat, it imitates the rhythm short-long of motif (a), though the accentuation is changed. In order to make this relation comprehensible the pianist should play the chord fairly well in time. Performers like to hesitate and to linger 'dreamily' on the notes in the mistaken intention of thus suggesting the character of the piece. But the dreaming need not be applied from outside; it is already in the music.

Motif (b) looks very different from (a), but the resumption of the interval C–F and the chord, again off the beat, give us a hint that the two motifs are related. In fact (b) is an elaborate and most interesting variation of (a).[1] The crotchet upbeat is transformed into an upbeat of five quavers which duplicate and telescope motif (a) in diminution (a[1]), while the 'strong beat' is transferred to the second crotchet, thus coinciding this time with the chord.

The F is reached without the weight of its first appearance, but this time it is emphasized by the subdominant chord—a fine example of a harmonic variation. (a) and (b) together form the first phrase (A) of the four-bar clause, whose continuity should not be broken by affected hesitation (the slur extending from the minim F indicates *legato*, but does not refer to the phrasing). The rise of the melody and the change of harmony on its repeated climax are the chief features of the structure; the shifting of the main stress is another; a further feature, to which Berg has drawn our attention, is the dissonant passing note E which always recurs in later variations of the clause. The E, since it is the start of the melody's rise, must be distinct without being stressed; the *arpeggio*-like continuation suggests the very slight acceleration of a *rubato obbligato*, but the important interval C–F must be in strict time again, to prepare the surprising climax of the phrase on the subdominant— dreamland reached without hesitations.

The second phrase (B) has a very different structure. It is immediately evident that the notes are grouped into shorter units and that the texture, essentially in four parts, is richer. These features make for diversity of colour and dynamics, but melodically the phrase is less emphatic than the first. The interval C–F of motif (c) discloses its relation to (b) and (a), and the surge upwards is resumed in (c[1])

[1] Alban Berg has analysed the whole of the *Träumerei* from a different angle. Unfortunately, his interesting article has never been published in English. The present analysis, intended for the performer, makes use of a few points from Berg's argument.

and ($c^2$). Yet the second phrase leads downward, by way of descending leaps placed between the motifs which should be distinctly phrased as units, (c) and ($c^1$) of half a bar each, ($c^2$) of one bar. The three motifs are closely related but their accentuations differ: (c) has a straight, though slight, accent on the strong beat (the different rhythmic significance of the notes C–F in bars two and three is a fine point); in ($c^1$), the change of harmony makes the first note, G, the melodic centre; in ($c^2$), the accentuation becomes ambiguous because of the growing prominence of the bass line: here again, a change of the harmony adds weight to the first note F; full texture, on the other hand, supports the rise of the melody until it falls back to G. The bass, linking this clause with the next, has meanwhile gained momentum, and there can be no doubt that its C must be the most prominent note of the dominant chord on the second beat. All dynamic inflexions are slight and subtle—Schumann indicates $p$, but very little else. The three motifs, gradually sinking lower, involve an overall *diminuendo* and the accents described above must be contained within the general decrease; the upward melodic turns, taken from the initial motif, subside—comparable, perhaps, to a look backward at parting.

Our findings are based on the structure of the four-bar clause and are likely to need modifications in accord with the music's further development. The clause is the antecedent of a period. The whole piece is formed as a ternary song and consists exclusively of variations on the clause we have analysed.

# IV. MOVEMENT

For music to become alive, the composer's plan has to be carried out. Making music means action on a prescribed course. The musical structure is so devised that, rightly understood, it directs not only the physical, but also the mental action of the performer. He should feel the groups of notes as latent forces; they are arranged in such a fashion that they create an impression of continually changing degrees of tension and relaxation, according to the affinity or disparity of the structural features. Potential energies are waiting to be released by the performer's action. Music, while it unfolds, is felt to be moving along. In the visible world, movement is the only condition in which the progress of time is directly perceptible. Applied to music, the term movement signifies a continuous change of sonorities.

### MOVEMENT AND TEMPO

We must distinguish between the notions 'movement' and 'tempo'. Not only the rhythm, but each change of pitch, each turn of the harmony, is felt as a source of movement. Even sustained notes 'move' as their dynamics or colour change. Tempo, on the other hand, should be understood as the average rate at which the movement proceeds. If we make this distinction, the relation between movement and tempo corresponds to that between rhythm and time, tempo being the measurement of movement as time is the measurement of rhythm.

### QUALITIES OF MOVEMENT

Movement is continuous but not uniform, coherent but

126

flexible. Naturally, movement can be quick or slow—which is not the same as quick and slow tempo. The movement may be quick in an *Adagio* and slow in an *Allegro*. The tempo of the *Figaro* overture is very fast, but the movement of the second subject is not.

*Mozart*, Le Nozze di Figaro, *K.492, Overture*

If we do not fear the whip of the tempo indication, *Presto*, but allow the tune to take its own natural pace, we realize that it does not move very quickly. The tempo does not appreciably slow down, but the smoothness of the structural proportions suggests leisure rather than haste. The melodic line is highly developed and makes no sense if it is hurried.

Movement is characterized by many qualities other than quick and slow; it may be steady or variable, urgent or deliberate, strained or relaxed, decisive or vague, energetic or languid, light or heavy. In other words, the character of the music is expressed in its movement. And, in turn, his realization of the structure will lead the performer to the correct kind of movement, as shown in the following examples.

## MOVEMENT AND STRUCTURE

We have analysed the first phrase of the finale of Mozart's piano quartet in G minor (cf. Ex. 30). If we compare the first phrase (A) with the second (B) we feel immediately that their movement differs in character. The first phrase is essentially deliberate, while in the second we feel a sense of urgency. Let us try to find the structural features which make for either of these qualities, deliberation or urgency.

Clearly, the first phrase is highly organized, in contrast to the second, which is rhythmically uniform. The upbeat of motif (a) starts to play on and about the note D; ornamental quavers and subsequent crotchets, rebounding as it were from the repeated Ds, serve as a spring-board from which the melody leaps to G. Disjunct motion continues in the second bar and its distinctly melodic character tends to move at a leisurely pace; but it would be wrong to linger unduly on the minim C (no *tenuto*!)—the melody would lose its momentum too early. The initial drive must carry the movement into the third bar, in which the chromatic harmony provides a fresh impulse—rhythmic, melodic and harmonic elements in turn contribute to the pace of the movement. By the way, the rhythmic contraction of the fourth bar is also melodically a contraction: the principal notes of the opening B–D–G, transposed to the dominant, form the third motif F♯–A–D.

A moment of tension results from the abrupt ending of the first phrase and the subsequent rest, which, in order to keep the movement active, has to be given less than its full value. The second phrase consists of motif (a¹)—derived from (a)—which is developed by way of a sequence. We feel that the rising repetitions of the motif drive forward to the melodic apex, B; but the drive abates with the change of direction of the melodic line and the cadence in the seventh and eighth bars. The various features of the first phrase balance each other; the repetitions in the second phrase drive the movement forward.

Often the impulse of the movement changes within a phrase and even within a group of equal note-values. The performer is not always aware of the little inflexions he is applying, of those minute accelerations or moments of hesitation, the shortening or stressing of a note or two, which I shall call *rubato obbligato*. In our Mozart example, the quavers of the second phrase are not meant to be played evenly—the groups which they form would not be understood if they were not slightly separated from each other. Quite instinctively, the performer plays the first two notes of each group quicker than the second two—each group of four notes consists of an upbeat and an *appoggiatura*. The dissonances of the *appoggiaturas* are stressed, while the chromatic passing notes are slightly hurried. Minute though these rhythmic inflexions are, it is worth the performer's while to be conscious of what he is doing instinctively.

The first phrase begins steadily—but only for the first two notes. If we listen carefully to what the structure reveals, we feel already, after the second note C, an urge towards the chromatic C♯, while the *appoggiatura* E (so far, the melodic climax) steadies the movement. The first crotchet D rapidly follows the preceding quavers, and the rebounding crotchets move sufficiently fast to sustain the drive towards G. The G provides a momentary respite and is certainly a longer crotchet than the preceding D, but the minim C is hardly twice as long.

So far our analysis reveals that highly organized structures require a more deliberate movement than simple ones; that rhythmic variety is likely to give rise to *rubato obbligato*; that a rise of the melodic line can increase the movement—if no other structural features contradict it; that rests must be timed with discretion in order to keep the movement in being; that repetition can increase the movement's momentum, but not necessarily its speed: the character of the repeated shape remains preserved. The repetitions of the rising motif (a¹) (Ex. 30) urge the movement on, but the repetition of motif (b) stresses the melodic character of the first phrase.

There is a certain similarity of structure shared by the second phrase of the Mozart theme and that of the finale of Beethoven's second symphony (cf. Ex. 27). As a result of the changing size and direction of the intervals, however, the melodic line of the quavers is more developed in Beethoven's tune. In consequence, and in spite of a tempo that is much faster than Mozart's, the movement does not convey the same sense of urgency, but suggests an evenly flowing motion.

### CONTRAST DOES NOT INTERRUPT THE MOVEMENT

The two phrases of the Beethoven theme, one of two, the other of four bars, are dissimilar in almost every respect. The melodic line, rhythm, texture, dynamics, accentuation —everything changes after the first two bars; tempo and key remain almost the only common features. Nevertheless, the *piano* phrase is not a new start, but a continuation of the *forte* phrase. The first impulse must still be active and the sudden change from force to brilliant grace must find the players' minds flexible enough to adapt themselves to the new mood. They must begin with great energy and change their attack[1] rapidly. The tempo remains the same, but the movement changes. It deprives the theme of its character if the contrast between *forte* and *piano* is ironed out (as is often the case). When, in the consequent, the unison passage recurs, Beethoven marks it, not *forte*, but *fortissimo*, thus emphasizing the importance of the dynamic contrast.

---

[1] It is, of course, only the strings, with the emphasis on the first violins, who really have to change the quality of their attack. But if the rest of the orchestra do not perceive the contrasting elements that go to make up the theme, they cannot understand the parts they themselves have to play.

## THE DRAMATIC ELEMENT

The performer needs an actor's gift for identifying himself with the character he has to present. Instrumental as well as vocal music contains a dramatic element. With the singer it is, of course, both the words and the music that give his performance dramatic character; he has to enact the music, not only the words, and should beware lest the words, instead of enhancing the music, destroy it.

Singers often like to stress the verbal meaning beyond its due. They commit the serious blunder of shaping sentences of speech instead of phrases of music, of making points that are not suggested by the melody. In a good song, everything the composer intends to express is implied in the music. Whatever correspondence with the words he means to establish is embodied in the structure of melody and accompaniment. The singer must realize the musical form, i.e., perform, no less faithfully than the instrumentalist. The only difference rests in the words, the additional guide the singer has to help him find the music's character.

In Schumann's song *Der arme Peter*, the singer represents a poor lad whose sweetheart has married another man. When looking at the music, the singer will immediately discover a certain correspondence between music and words. The narrow intervals of the quaver motion suggest the pangs of heartache, the subsequent rise to E, and later to G, an emotional outburst. But the musical structure indicates what is required of the performer in far greater detail than do the words. The melody is a period of eight bars, whose principal feature is the juxtaposition of conjunct and disjunct motion. Motif (a) tends upwards in conjunct motion, but its rise is immediately reversed, frustrated as it were, and the line circles round the note B. The insistently recurring B's produce a moment of tension, which is released by the melody's disjunct rise to E, the line then resuming its initial direction. There are two motifs, (a) and (b), whose structural functions are diametrically opposed. While the exact

131

Schumann, Song, 'Der arme Peter II'

repetitions of (a) keep the structure loose (cf. Chapter III, pp. 83–84), the variation of (b) unites not only the second phrase, but the whole clause of four bars.

The accentuation of the melody is still more varied. In the antecedent, the repetition of the B's lends a slight weight to almost every crotchet, but the broadening rhythm of the second phrase (B) accentuates only the first beats, the notes E and C. In the consequent, on the other hand, the melody comes to rest on a minim B before it rises, now without an upbeat, to the climax G. The minim B, and the lack of a preparatory upbeat to the second phrase, make, in retro-spect, a compact unit of the first phrase and separate it from the second, which functions as a strongly emphasized conclusion to the whole eight-bar period. The main accent of the second clause is on the first G, a lesser one on F♯, and that on E is within a *diminuendo*.

The different structures of antecedent and consequent give rise to different accentuations. Whether the singer realizes the implications of the structure by intuition or analysis, varied ways of phrasing and accentuation are necessary for putting the music's character across. Uniform

*Verdi*, Aida, *1st act, duet, Amneris and Radames*

accents dull the music. Nor should the singer endeavour to stress the *W* of the word *Weh* (woe)—the resulting extra accent would spoil the tune's rhythmic balance.

An interesting similarity to Schumann's song may be found in an instrumental passage from Verdi's *Aida*— another tune which is meant to express jealousy (66).

The very quick tempo, Allegro agitato presto, must still be sufficiently spacious for implementing the structure, otherwise the rhythm is deprived of its cutting edge. The rhythm and melodic line of the five quaver upbeats, oscillating between B and A♯, become mere ornaments if the conductor's too hasty beat leaves no time for the execution of very short *staccatos*. The movement, though rapid, must allow for the articulation of every note.

## MOVEMENT IS SUBORDINATE TO THE STRUCTURE

The character of the right movement cannot be gauged from the melody alone, but only from the whole structure. If we try to find structural features that make for certain qualities of movement we shall have to bear in mind that other features may, in fact, prevail, which exert the opposite influence. The tune from *Aida*, for example, could move faster than the metronome figure indicates without its line and rhythm becoming incomprehensible, though the long upbeat adds an element of heaviness. But if we consider the elaborate texture of the accompaniment, which keeps every quaver vibrating, we fully understand the harassing, but not hurrying, character of the movement.

A structure like the opening of the *Figaro* overture, on the other hand, would be meaningless in the tempo of the *Aida* tune, ♩ = 132. The rate of exposition would be slower than our ability to hear it, a case of bad timing. The tune falls easily on the ear, because the music is gradually exposed in rhythmic units of one, two and four bars, and the melodic line gradually developed by repeatedly resuming earlier patterns.

## MOVEMENT IN QUICK PASSAGES

Runs, figures and other shapes that contain equal note-values in quick succession, are sometimes difficult to control. By nature, movement tends to increase its momentum, and the performer tends to hurry, often without being aware of it. We must distinguish between an increase of movement that is based on the musical structure and one that is caused by the mechanism of the performer's mind or body. Repeated patterns may sometimes legitimately be felt as driving forward, but at the moment the structure changes —though the note-values remain the same—the movement must be directed anew. The third prelude from the *Forty-Eight* will show us how a subtle change of movement can be effected.

*Bach*, The Well-Tempered Clavier, *Book I, Prelude in C sharp*

The music will sound artificially restrained if the performer does not allow the figures to flow easily; it will become stiff if he steadies the rhythm by accentuating the beats. But from the sixth bar, the changed melodic line gives the movement a new direction. Disjunct motion gives way to conjunct, and hurrying would blur the melodic design. Clarity of line can only be obtained if the two melodic turns, F♯–E♯–D♯ and F♯–D♯–E♯, are kept distinct. The drive, natural to the first five bars, must cease in the sixth—without the tempo being changed.

Equal note-values do not necessarily give rise to rhythmic uniformity, still less to uniformity of movement. The melodic design and its harmonic implications may be a source of rhythmic variety even within a line of equal semi-quavers. Schubert's *Moment Musical* in C sharp minor is a

*Schubert*, Moment Musical, *Op. 94, No. 4 in C sharp minor*

case in point. Many pianists fail to recognize the music's wayward character because they mistake the semiquaver motion for *moto perpetuo*. The melodic line is highly developed and makes for varied, if subtle, rhythmic groupings and stresses. There are several distinctive features:

(1) the zigzag line, whose alternating directions must remain distinct throughout;

(2) the interval of a third, which moves both ways down and up, and becomes prominent in bar 7, while later on, in bar 15, it appears inverted as a sixth;

(3) the mainly disjunct motion;

(4) the irregular change of harmony;

(5) the changing harmonic relations between the two strands of the texture: virtually unison at the beginning, they vary in subsequent bars. After the upbeat, the notes seem to be grouped into a pattern of four semiquavers, but the change of harmony on the last quavers of bars 1 and 2 (A and G♯ respectively) suggests that the phrasing should maintain the initial upbeat. In fact, the line is a composite one, whose elements contradict each other, and the ambiguity which results must be preserved by playing at a speed (*Moderato!*) at which it comes across. Neither the repeated patterns, nor the upbeats, require anything more emphatic than clear articulation of every note; on the other hand, the movement must take account of structural changes. The first two bars form a rhythmic unit, but in the third bar the top notes E and C♯, which are not, as before, anticipated by the left hand, need a little stressing. In the fourth bar, the conjunct motion of the passing note must be deliberate. Then, with increased movement, the line surges upwards. But it recoils dissonantly from the climactic G♯, and, while the movement recedes, hovers around the intervals of a third, with slight accents on the quaver beats of bar 7. In bar 8, conjunct motion restores the steady pace of the opening. It is understood that drive and recoil, stresses and accents, should not disrupt the continuity of the line, but should realize the diversity of the structure by the smallest possible inflexions of rhythm and dynamics.

Downward direction of the line does not always imply a

decrease of movement. The descending scale that opens the D minor prelude from the second volume of the *Forty-Eight* is felt to be the source of an impetuous drive by virtue

**Bach**, The Well-Tempered Clavier, *Book II, Prelude in D minor*

Ex.69

of several structural features: its place at the beginning of the piece, the tonic which it represents, and the clear-cut rhythm with which it starts. The subsequent repeated figures keep the first impulse in being until, in the fifth bar, the scale recurs; and throughout the prelude it is either the downward scale or figures derived from it that renew the movement's drive. Rhythmically, the first bar is a kind of upbeat to the repeated pattern, but dynamically, the first D is the centre of gravity. Melodic, rhythmic, harmonic and dynamic components of the structure are often differently centred—diversity of features contributes to the interest of the music, but poses difficult problems for the performer. We have seen that in Schubert's *Moment Musical* (cf. Ex. 68) the melody pivots on two different hinges.

### AN EXAMPLE OF VAGUE MOVEMENT

After Bach's heavy 'upbeat', an example of a very light

downbeat. In Debussy's Prelude *La fille aux cheveux de lin*, the melody seems to drift along until it comes to rest on the

Debussy, Preludes *for Pianoforte, Book I, 'La fille aux cheveux de lin'*

chord of the subdominant. An impression of movement without direction is suggested by several features of the structure: the line, undulating between Db and Eb; uniform rhythm, not yet committed to motivic development; and ambiguity of harmony. The 'tempo' indication *Très calme et doucement expressif* does not describe the tempo (which is given by a metronome figure) but the character of the movement. In order to convey the impression of great calmness, the music must be played without either haste or hesitation. The words *doucement expressif* refer to both the pianist's touch and the general style of performance; they ask, in particular, for distinctly soft degrees of dynamics. And *sans rigueur* indicates that the square-looking rhythm of quavers and semiquavers should be deprived of its edge.

Most important for the start of the *p-legato* melody is the weight of the sustained Db. It must be prevented from sounding isolated, but felt as moving towards the notes that follow. To this effect, the pianist must give the first note the fulness of tone of the Db and sustain it at the *piano ordinario* level. Any further accents, especially on the second Db and Eb, would disrupt the movement's smoothness. The first Eb, the lowest note of the line, stands out by its very nature, similarly the last Gb under the first slur.

If the unaccompanied passage is imagined as resting on the chord of the subdominant (which enters only later), unwarranted accents will more easily be avoided.

The tenuto mark on the G♮ under the second slur—it is still the same phrase—is a little stress without accent, emphasizing the inversion of the preceding motif. The stress as well as the hairpin imply that there should be neither accent nor stress on the tonic chord of the downbeat—the melody remains afloat.

### MOVEMENT OF SUSTAINED NOTES

A sustained note that stands at the beginning of a phrase without being part of a motif, must nevertheless be felt as moving. Its tone volume and colour should make the following notes sound like an inevitable continuation. In order to achieve this aim, the performer must have a clear conception of the whole phrase in his mind before he strikes the sustained note.

*Beethoven, Piano Sonata in C, Op. 2, No. 3, 1st mvt.*

To keep the opening phrase of Beethoven's piano sonata (Op. 2, No. 3) moving, the semiquaver motif must follow before the impact of the first minim is spent (cf. Ex. 71). How to keep the sound alive is the problem that sustained notes or chords present. Fulness of tone naturally contributes to the duration of the impact. The impact of *forte* lasts longer than that of *piano*, longer still if it comes from a full chord than from a single note. Especially on the piano, timing and dynamics of *sostenutos* must be adjusted.

## AN EXAMPLE OF DECIDED MOVEMENT

The instrumental introduction to *Enthauptung* (Decapitation), a number from Schoenberg's *Pierrot lunaire*, is an unusual structure, but not just because of the dissonances of

**Schoenberg**, Pierrot lunaire, *Op. 21, 13th piece, 'Enthauptung'*

the texture or as an example of tone painting. The melodic line of the 'cello climbs within three bars through more than three octaves and descends from the climactic G$\sharp$ through a similar compass within a single bar. The movement has great drive, if it is correctly performed.

It is the rhythmic development of motif (a) that secures continuity. In order to cohere, the huge intervals must be clearly articulated. This motif (a) is twice repeated, the second time in reversed rhythm (a$^1$)—the long note becomes an upbeat to the short one. In the following phrase (B), the three notes of the motif go to develop different rhythms: (a$^2$), (a$^3$) and (a$^4$).

The rapid leaps of (a) are the cause of the initial drive, but the player must already feel, and convey during the opening, sustained E$\flat$, an urge towards the notes that follow it, anticipating the trend of the movement before it is revealed. The reason for a performer's action is always shown by what comes after. On the B$\flat$, again, the movement towards D$\flat$ should be felt. The movement does not only connect the motifs, but goes from one note to the other, from motif to motif. The breaks for changing the bow must be as short as possible. That the movement is from note to note is still more evident in the second bar, in which the *crescendo* during the dotted minim D maintains the melody's vitality. The rhythm of the accompaniment supports the drive, especially in the second and third bars.

### STRUCTURE AND MOVEMENT

From our analysis we can deduce a few more principles.

Movement connects the notes. Each note moves to the next. If they are separated by rests, a moment of tension or relaxation—as the case may be—must be felt.

*Rubato* is caused by contradictory tendencies of structural features. The degree of *rubato*—whether it should be *rubato obbligato* or more elaborate—depends on the amount of contradictory features; and on the performer's ability to reconcile them convincingly.

The character of movement is chiefly determined by the rhythmic, melodic and harmonic features of the passage.

Conjunct motion moves more easily than disjunct, but large intervals at reasonable speed may impart great impetus to the movement (cf. Ex. 72; also Ex. 3 and the beginning of Ex. 27).

Changes in the structural features are likely to alter the trend of the movement, but need not change the tempo.


### REPETITION AND SEQUENCE

If many, all, or the most significant features of the structure change, the new structure must be presented with relative deliberation—contrasts are not meant to be neglected. Repetitions, on the other hand, and slight variations of structural features tend to ease the movement. In particular, sequences of short patterns very often create a sense of urgency. In such instances it is harmony that sets the pace, while the repeated rhythmic and melodic pattern needs no further explicitness.

A sense of urgency can be felt in slow as well as in quick tempo.

In the example from *Tristan*, the movement begins to drive forward with the shortening of phrase (B) and especially during the sequence of the last two bars. The impulse of the repeated pattern in Ex. 74 is evident. Contractions of the model in sequences contribute greatly to a movement's drive. Development sections of sonata movements and sentence-like structures (cf. Ex. 43) offer an abundance of examples.

A drive forward is less felt in sequences whose melody is highly organized, such as for instance the phrase (A) of Ex. 73. The model consists of two contrasting motifs, (a) and (b), the first leaping down the characteristic interval of a seventh, the second rising in conjunct motion; while the first comprises only half a bar, the second extends to one-and-a-half bars. During the sequential repeat the interest

143

## Wagner, Tristan und Isolde, *Prelude*

remains still concentrated on the composite structure of the model.

*Richard Strauss*, Der Rosenkavalier, *Op. 59, Introduction*

Repetitions of a short pattern without development of harmony are likely to create a moment of tension which increases as the repetitions continue. Climaxes of this kind are sometimes built on a pedal, like the transition from the scherzo to the finale of Beethoven's fifth symphony or the *crescendo* in the exposition of the third *Leonora* overture. In his seventh symphony, Beethoven builds the coda of the first movement on an *ostinato* bass figure, on top of which variations on a simple phrase grow to a climax. Pedals are likely to create a feeling of tension—one component of the structure remains fixed, as it were, while the others move forward. In introductory passages they rouse the expectation of things to come, or a feeling of suspense (cf. the beginning of the *St. Matthew Passion*).

*Johann Strauss, Waltz, Op. 314, 'The Blue Danube'*

A chain of slightly varied repetitions may produce the impression of accumulating energies, as in Johann Strauss's famous waltz (75).

The *Blue Danube* waltz is a sentence-like structure whose basic model, a phrase of four bars, consists of two duetting strands; the alternation of tonic and dominant balances the form and groups the repeated phrases symmetrically into clauses of eight bars. After the third clause—i.e., after the fifth repetition of the model phrase—the movement's accumulated force drives the melody up to its melodic climax.

Repetitions of motifs and phrases influence the movement in many different ways, by relaxing or tightening the structure, keeping the form loose, as in sequences and sentences, or balancing and closing it, as in symmetrical structures. Harmony plays an important part, by way of modulations and cadences, in directing the movement. A repeated cadence-like formula at the end of a piece heightens the impression of finality.

## MOVEMENT IN SLOW TEMPO

In slow as well as in moderate and fast tempo, movement must remain flexible; in fact, a slow piece is likely to include a greater diversity of features and to require a more explicit *rubato* than a fast one. Though restfulness is their predominant characteristic, slow movements often grow very lively during subsidiary passages. The bridge section of the Andante from the *Jupiter* symphony, for example, is surprisingly agitated. In slow introductory sections, on the other hand, the movement usually maintains a somewhat dragging character.

## INCREASE OF MOVEMENT THROUGH THE DEVELOPMENT OF MOTIFS

The first part of the sixth symphony of Tchaikovsky shows changes of movement which are caused by the development of the principal theme. An adagio introduction presents the theme's first motif, (a) in Ex. 76b, in slow and sombre character. There is an increase of dynamics during the first sequences, but no sense of urgency is felt. The low range of the texture, soft dynamics and darkness of timbre (double bass and bassoon) suggest heaviness, and the sluggish chromatic descent of the bass adds to the impression of inertia. Even without the indication ♩ = 54 the intelligent musician would infer the required slowness from the features of the structure (cf. Ex. 76a).

*Tchaikovsky, Symphony No. 6 in B minor, Op. 74, 1st mvt.*

(c)

When the Allegro non troppo begins, the principal theme
appears in the shape of Ex. 76b. Its first motif is har-
monized as a cadence to the dominant and forms the treble
of four, smoothly moving parts, which distribute one chord
to every note. By this structural elaboration the motif gains
shape and the movement is given direction. Motif (b) is a

149

variation of motif (a) and develops the structure further: the varied upbeat splits the one motif into two and adds momentum to the movement of the first phrase (A). The second phrase (B) repeats motif (c), which is derived from (a¹); in semiquavers throughout, the phrase is an antithesis of the first. Together, the two phrases form a clause of four bars which is repeated, almost like the antecedent of a period. Rests are a significant feature of the theme—it begins in fits and starts. Nevertheless the movement must be felt to proceed and, for this purpose, the rests must be kept in time.

After its first exposition, the rhythmic structure of the theme is radically changed by omission of the second phrase (cf. Ex. 76c). A sequence is built, in the course of which the rests, separating the motifs (a) and (b), are discarded. The growing, ever-tighter rhythm is felt to drive the movement irresistibly forward.

## RITARDANDO

There are many sources which slacken or retard the movement, apart from such relaxation as is provided by rhythmic symmetry, antithetical phrases, or cadences and cadence-like turns. Here, the complex question of the function and scope of *ritardandos* arises.

*Ritardandos* are always—or always should be—a consequence of the musical structure. They occur most frequently at the end of a piece, or as preparation for a recapitulation or new section; often they support a transition to a slower, or faster, tempo. Otherwise, *ritardandos* occur chiefly for harmonic or dynamic reasons. They emphasize certain features of the structure.

Beethoven's eighth symphony is in F major, but the second theme of the first movement is presented in the major of the submediant, before it is repeated on the dominant. It is the short and somewhat abrupt modulation from D to C, which requires a broadening of the sixth bar.

Beethoven, Symphony No. 8 in F, Op. 93, 1st mvt.

The modulating sequence of motif (b) introduces the note
E♭ as a stranger, and it needs a moment's thought to understand the E♭ as component of a diminished seventh chord

which leads to the dominant of C. The question of how great the *ritardando* should be is answered by the proportions of the rhythmic structure. The two clauses, the first in D, the second in C, must be felt as units of contrasts—not only different keys but also different orchestral *timbres*. The E♭ is the crucial note which, almost as a second thought, turns to the dominant; it, and the subsequent D, both belong to motif (b), and should be separated as little as possible—the E♭ must be sustained up to *a tempo*. When the *ritardando* recurs in the C major clause in different harmonic surroundings, it introduces a new section which changes the movement's character.

Contrasting dynamics require a *ritardando* in the theme of Beethoven's piano sonata, Op. 111. After the violent *ff*

Beethoven, Piano Sonata No. 32 in C minor, Op. 111, 1st mvt.

of the opening, the *mezzo-piano* repetition of the second motif (b) requires slower movement, otherwise it will sound like a wholly uncharacteristic anti-climax.

The abbreviation *rit.* may stand for either *ritardando* or *ritenuto*—the two terms are often confused by composers and performers alike. *Ritardando* slows down gradually, *ritenuto* holds back from the beginning. The distinction is sometimes a very subtle one, and the varying degrees of either *ritardando* or *ritenuto* can be judged only on the merits of each case. The passage from Beethoven's sonata,

marked *poco ritenente*, is *ritenuto* rather than *ritardando*—
to be held back, but not further slowed down, since that
would deprive the theme of its momentum.

The phrasing of *ritardandos* is sometimes difficult, for the
retardation should not distort the proportions of the structure. Our example from Beethoven's eighth symphony is a
case in point: the E♮ should not be closely linked with the
preceding notes, but slightly separated from them—it belongs to the *a tempo* continuation. Undue hesitation on the
preceding D is fatal. The expression *cédez* would perhaps
suggest the degree of retardation needed in the passage.
*Cédez* is a very suggestive term; it means: yield to the
requirements of the structure. And it implies: do not try to
enforce an unnatural steadiness on the movement. The
English expression 'take your time' is less precise, and does
not really mean the same.

A passage from the Andante of Schubert's piano sonata
in E flat, Op. 122, includes a *ritardando* that is a result of

Schubert, Piano Sonata in E flat, Op. 122, 2nd mvt.

both harmonic (modulation) and dynamic (*pp*) features.
It is a true *ritardando*—the shape of the melody allows for

153

slowing down gradually. The tender expressiveness of the
phrase is almost dramatic, but should not induce the performer to exaggerate the retardation. The degree of permissible slowness is limited by the necessity of keeping the
movement alive. Standing between two very short pauses
the phrase is in parenthesis; it is the more necessary to preserve the context by sensitive timing of both *ritardando* and
pauses.

### THE PAUSE

A pause is a temporary halt, but should not convey the
impression of movement having ceased altogether. Except
at the end of a piece, a pause is meant to rouse the listener's
expectation and thus to create a moment of tension. In a
sense, it is comparable to the colon of speech.[1] Like *ritardandos*, pauses often stand at the close of a section, as a
transition to a new tempo or new character of movement.
Pauses at the beginning stress the preliminary character of
an introduction whose movement is still undecided. Sometimes a pause emphasizes a dynamic or harmonic surprise
(Haydn!). The duration of the halt, and whether there
ought to be a gap or comma after it, can only be read from
the context. Pauses must be well timed—dramatically as it
were—but the widespread opinion that they ought to be

---

[1] The traditional halt before a cadenza in concertos is a typical
instance of a musical colon, pointing at the things to come. Pauses
towards the end of an aria were formerly meant to be ornamented by
the singer. We have become purists in this respect—not without
justification—and do not want to hear more notes or notes other than
the composer has written. Yet these pauses sometimes look puzzling,
like those in the third bar before the end of Susanna's aria 'Deh vieni'
(from *Figaro*); at this point, the melody, as it stands, amounts almost
to an anti-climax. Remembering C. P. E. Bach's words that no singer
would dare to sustain a note without embellishment, we may wonder
how the sustained F, two bars earlier, was dealt with in Mozart's
time. But who today would dare and try to find the notes to suit the
perfection of the music? In my youth I heard Cherubino's aria 'Non so
più' sung with a top B♮ in the last bar but one. It sounded horribly
out of style.

'in time', i.e., that their duration is doubled, or prolonged by half of, or double, the note's value, is wrong. No hard and fast rule is applicable, except that the pause should *not* be 'in time' in this sense.

There is hardly a composer in whose works pauses occur as frequently as in Beethoven's—they are typical of his incisive style. At the opening of his fifth symphony, the pauses are components of the structure and as important as the rhythm and the interval of the motif's vigorous announcement in *ff*. The unison of the orchestra contributes to the introductory character of the opening bars—the key is not yet established and E flat might still be the tonic. As for the duration of the pauses, opinions differ. Wagner wanted them sustained 'long and awesomely', but, surely, they should not last so long that the movement's continuity is lost? Even during the pauses the movement must be felt and should not be allowed to flag before the motif is developed in soft dynamics. On the other hand, the pauses should not make the impression of being 'in time'. Both

*Beethoven, Symphony No. 6 in F (Pastoral), Op. 68, 1st mvt.*

the *ff* repetition and the *p* continuation are surprises and must be timed as such. The *p* passage replaces the vigour of the preceding introduction by refinement—defined articulation and clear tone.

The pause at the opening of one *Pastoral* symphony (Ex. 80) has a similar introductory function but means something different.

It stands at the end of a four-bar clause whose structure is unusual. Three contrasting motifs (a), (b), and (c), are combined, but their grouping makes for rhythmic ambiguity. The lower C is part of motif (b), but it is also heard as an upbeat to (c). Still more interesting, the rhythm of the clause has a suggestion of 3/4 time about it (with the second bar line shifted a crotchet later). Thus conceived, the clause comprises not three motifs, but only one. In fact, it is a closely woven melody and forms a kind of antecedent of an eight-bar sentence that is interrupted by the pause. At the opening of the fifth symphony, a sixteen-bar sentence gains shape only after the pause; but in Ex. 80 a

Beethoven, Symphony No. 5 in C minor, Op. 67, 3rd mvt.

solidly constructed clause is placed before the pause, while afterwards the structure becomes loose. Further on, and throughout the first movement, the music develops at a leisurely pace. But the first four bars give its essence in a kind of motto.

In the scherzo of the fifth symphony (81), a pause balances the second phrase with the first.

It is utterly wrong to give more emphasis to the second phrase than its structure allows. The first phrase is highly characteristic in melodic and harmonic respects, but the second is not, and becomes inflated if the movement is prematurely held back. As an antithesis to the first it would carry little weight without the prolongation of the dominant chord, which stresses the key of C minor against the preceding F♯ (and later F♯ and C♯) of the modulating first phrase. The pause is introduced by a *poco rit.*, and the character of the music reminds us of a remark by C. P. E. Bach:[1] 'In approaching a pause which expresses lassitude, tenderness or sadness, it is usual to hold the time back a little.'

A pause is often, though not always, introduced by a *ritardando*. A little *cédez* sounds natural in the third bar of the *Pastoral* symphony (cf. Ex. 80), but only during the three quavers. Any further delay on the semiquavers would distort the motif's character—its structure would become incomprehensible. *Ritardandos* should never be automatic; they broaden the movement gradually, but the proportions of the structure must remain recognizable.

Slowing down before a halt is a natural process. Force is needed for ending a movement abruptly, but force is a quality not unknown in music. There is no scope for a *ritardando* in the opening bar of the fifth symphony; nor should the *ff* quavers be slower than the principal tempo.

In the finale of the *Eroica*, the pause within the theme must be treated with discretion (cf. Ex. 82). The three abrupt *f* strokes and the pause on the subsequent *p* are

[1] Ibid.

Beethoven, Symphony No. 3 in E flat (Eroica), Op. 55, 4th mvt.

structural features that balance each other: a single note in
*p*, against three in *f*, needs a prolongation which, however,
must be short, otherwise the rhythmic structure becomes
unbalanced. There is no structural reason for a *ritardando*
before the pause, except perhaps, in the first variation (a
slight *cédez* before the *appoggiatura*). In particular, a
retardation during the semiquavers of the fully organized
theme can easily disrupt the structure (e.g., bars 92–95). On
the other hand, some of the Variations for piano (Op. 35), on
the same theme, require a *ritardando* for the sake of certain
melodic, harmonic and textural features which prepare the
recurring pause. The Variations make a splendid subject for

study of the varying durations of pauses and varying degrees of *ritardandos*.

The application of the term *movement* to a piece of music indicates that we feel the piece as a whole. But fundamentally different methods are needed for shaping the form at large (i.e., its architecture) and its tiny, significant details, methods which sometimes seem to contradict each other. The 'big sweep' of a movement should not prevent the minute execution of the design, yet the performer is sometimes faced with the dilemma that the exigencies of the large form are at variance with those of the smaller units. In most cases, however, the dilemma is of his own making. He has, perhaps, fallen in love with a certain manner of phrasing, or with an over-characterization of a passage, which makes the piece fall 'to pieces'. A remedy may be found if subtler rhythmic or dynamic inflexions are employed or a climax, perhaps, allowed to grow on a bigger scale. If in the end the rival claims remain, the exigencies of the large form must prevail. Nevertheless, the performer must begin by considering the details and later try to co-ordinate them. His first task is to realize the character of the shapes, and to establish the appropriate movement.

## ORGANIZATION DEFINES THE MOVEMENT

The degree to which the performer's task is defined depends on the music's structural organization. If this is as complex as in Exx. 30, 46 and 50, the character of the music is unequivocally embodied in the structure. Variety of both melodic design and rhythmic grouping is the most significant feature of highly organized music. Rhythms which include various note-values contribute to a movement's definition, because the relation between long and short notes limits the possible durations of either. Harmonic features are sometimes paramount, as in the chorale (Ex. 53), but they leave the movement a considerable margin if the distribution of the harmony does not outline differ-

entiated rhythmic patterns. We have observed the influence
of textural (cf. Ex. 66) and dynamic features (cf. Ex. 27)
on a movement's character. The more defined the structure,
the less latitude is left for the performer's interpretation.
Too many points are fixed for allowing much difference of
opinions, though there is always scope for a performer's
imaginative penetration.

Music which is loosely constructed gives the performer
more freedom. Much vocal music comes into this category.
Strophic songs, in particular, allow the singer to vary the
expression, and even the phrasing, of the stanzas. In opera,
musical form is subject to the drama; the form of recitatives
is given by the words, and on many occasions the music
flexibly follows the dramatic action. Phrases are often short
and adaptable, as Wagner's *Leitmotifs* show. It is the same
in symphonic poems and other descriptive music. Ex. 83a is
meant to portray a grimace of a rascal, Till Eulenspiegel,
but the motif appears in many other guises (cf. Ex. 83b).

*Richard Strauss*, Till Eulenspiegel, *Op. 28*:

These examples are like the variations of Berlioz's *idée fixe*
(cf. Ex. 41 A–D).

Of course, a good vocal melody, though more loosely constructed, can be as highly organized as an instrumental one.

And the organization of musical form in opera needs great ingenuity if it is to satisfy both musical and dramatic requirements.

Music of the popular type is not often highly organized. Folk tunes give the singer's interpretative gift a wide scope. Catches are usually based on a single, but memorable, turn of the melody. The form of dances is defined more by specific movements of the body than by features of the structure. Jazz, in spite of its rhythmic intricacies, is not highly organized in melody. And the Viennese waltz, on which Johann Strauss lavished his rich melodic invention, is primitive in harmony.

# V. PHRASING

To a certain extent, phrasing is comparable to the delivery of speech. The speaker groups and shades the accentuations of the words according to sense; similarly the musical performer groups and diversely accentuates the notes that form musical shapes. The division of shapes corresponds to the punctuation of speech.

## PUNCTUATION

Rests between phrases are commas. Since they function as punctuation, the performer must time them independently of their note-values (cf. Chapter II/2, p. 46). Sometimes, the performer has to insert a minute breath, amounting to a slight comma, in order to make the division of rhythmic structures clear. Such commas are necessary, for instance, in Ex. 48, after the first and second phrases, otherwise the sequence of three crotchets (G–D–G and B♭-G-D) will obscure the fact that the second G and the D are upbeats.

In general, long units require a more distinct separation from each other than short ones: the comma will have to be more marked after a clause than after a phrase, more emphatic after, say, a period than after its antecedent. In Ex. 45, for instance, the quaver rest ( × ) after the first phrase (bar 2) should be shorter than that after the second (bar 4). However, the infinite variety of rhythmic structures defies generalization. There are many instances in which joints between units are screened by passing notes (cf. Ex. 46, bar 5), by a cadence (cf. Ex. 54, bars 4–5), or by other features, such as the repetition of motif (a) in the second bar of Ex. 28.

Rhythmic symmetry, melodic patterns and any kind of structural contrast make for the grouping of rhythmic units. There is no need for a comma where the phrases are sufficiently defined. Economy in applying the means of phrasing must be one of the performer's leading principles. No comma is needed in Ex. 26 after the first phrase (in bar 2), because the large interval of a sixth, unusual in the context, separates the phrases sufficiently.

Within swiftly moving patterns of equal note-values, the phrases cannot be separated by commas. In Exx. 67 and 69, rhythmic units of eight and four bars, respectively, are formed by textural contrasts. That a succession of equal notes can form a highly organized melody, is shown in Ex. 68 (cf. Chapter IV, pp. 136–137). The surge of the melody in bar 5 contrasts with the line of the preceding phrases; it is a new departure, that starts the second of two four-bar clauses. A *crescendo* will inevitably result from the melodic rise, and likewise a *diminuendo* from the descent in bar 8; thus the second clause will be further distinguished from the first by a dynamic feature.

If there is no rest, the time that is needed for a comma is usually taken from a fraction of the preceding note (as in Ex. 48). Sometimes, however, a minute rest 'out of time' has to be inserted. The peculiar structure of Ex. 49 (cf. Chapter III, pp. 99–100) requires commas after both bars 2 and 5 and bars 3 and 6; the preceding minims, however, cannot be shortened, because they counterbalance the minims on the first beats of bars 1 and 4. The commas are, therefore, practically 'out of time'; the last among them will be the longest, those after bars 2 and 5 the shortest. Punctuation clarifies the lengths of rhythmic units.

Punctuation may either shorten (for instance in the fourth bar of Ex. 30) or prolong the value of a rest. In the theme of Mozart's G minor symphony (cf. Ex. 42), the crotchet rest after the first clause (bar 5) is a fraction longer than that after the first phrase (bar 3); the earlier rest is almost in time, the later slightly prolonged. On the other

hand, the corresponding rest in bar 9 is not to be stressed
—it occurs in a different context. Because of different texture (sustained bass) and colour (the high range of the
violins), the continuation (Y) provides sufficient contrast.

Commas or prolonged rests, accompanied by evenly
flowing figures, are instances of *rubato*. The old rule, that
the accompanist should not follow the soloist's *rubato*,
applies here as well. It does not mean that the accompanist
should keep time automatically; he, too, has to phrase his
figurations. Obviously the steady movement of the accompaniment must be discreetly adapted. In the case of the
G minor symphony, the commas of the melody take so little
time that the accompanying violas have no difficulty in
adapting themselves imperceptibly.

It goes without saying that commas do not interrupt the
music's movement. On the contrary, they create moments
of tension or expectation which connect the separate groups
to each other.

### RESTS WITH DIVERSE FUNCTIONS

The theme from César Franck's *Variations Symphoniques*,
for piano and orchestra, is an interesting rhythmic structure, whose many rests fulfil diverse structural functions—
they group the motifs as well as the phrases and clauses.

In view of the theme's highly organized structure, elaborate phrasing seems indispensable. Artistic economy, on the
other hand, requires that a theme to be varied should be
presented as palpably plain as possible—the composer's
direction *con simplicità* stresses the point. The performer's
task, then, is to apply the necessary rhythmic and dynamic
inflexions with great restraint, insensibly as it were. To
neglect them entirely would deprive the theme of its character, but too much emphasis on details would weaken the
theme's formal function as the subject of a variation movement.

We have a ternary form of eighteen bars, whose first part
comprises two four-bar clauses (A) and (B), the middle

**César Franck**, Variations Symphoniques, *for piano and orchestra*

section one four-bar clause, and the third part one six-bar clause. The structures of the clauses differ widely.

The first clause is a very compact statement, in which two contrasting phrases are juxtaposed. The first phrase is fairly loose, built as it is from motif (a) and its varied repetition, but the second phrase is a full cadence on the tonic which, in retrospect, tightens the form of the first clause. The rests in bars 1 and 2 must be considered as part of motif (a), which thus always stands out in relief from its surroundings. But the rest in bar 4 has a different function: it separates two clauses. A slight prolongation of the rest is needed, in order to distinguish it from those of motif (a) which, of course, ought to be strictly in time.

The second clause is more loosely built. After reaching its apex, the note E, the melodic line does not further develop, but circles round the note C♯; the harmony modulates (to the mediant region); and the two phrases of the clause are co-ordinated rather than contrasted. They are linked by the movement of the tenor part (left hand), which tends to shorten the rest in bar 6.

The rest in bar 8 separates the first part of the theme from its middle section (C). Nevertheless, the rest should be strictly in time—for various reasons. The interval E–C♯ with which clause (C) begins briefly echoes the melodic content of the preceding clause (B) (from E, the melodic apex, to C♯). A prolongation of the separating rest would not only counter this structural feature, but weakly stress the repeated C♯ on the chord of the mediant. The middle section is very loosely built and requires a certain amount of *rubato*, but should, for this very reason, begin squarely in time. Motif (a), in downward motion, is varied and developed by way of a sequence. The elaborate variation of (a)—an octave lower, and with heavier texture (a¹), in which the crotchet upbeat is replaced by three quavers, and the crotchet rest by a quaver rest—requires a slight broadening which will prolong, in particular, the quaver rests in bars 9 and 11. It is for the sake of rhythmic balance that the unvaried motif (a), especially its upbeat and the preceding crotchet rest, must be well in time, if not hurried. And this is another reason for not prolonging the rest in bar 8.

No comma is required before the last clause (bar 12), because the different texture provides sufficient distinction. Motif (a), on the other hand, now without its rest, and moving downward from E in disjunct motion, relates clause (D) with clause (C), in spite of their apparent structural contrast. Clause (D) is remarkable for the insertion of bars 15 and 16, which resume the motif's structural rests. Thus the clause consists of three phrases, $(d^1)$, $(d^2)$ and $(d^3)$; the second $(d^2)$, which links $(d^1)$ and $(d^3)$, grows from the sequence of $(d^1)$; together with the cadential phrase $(d^1)$, it forms a free recapitulation of the theme's very first clause, (A).

The different structures of the theme's four clauses make for different rhythmic groupings. Clause (A) consists of $2 \times 1$ bar$+2$ bars; clause (B) of $2 \times 2$ bars; clause (C) of $4 \times 1$ bars; and clause (D) of $3 \times 2$ bars. Harmonically (A) is a cadence, (B) a modulation, (C) a free sequence, and (D) an exact sequence followed by a cadence.

## PUNCTUATION AND BREATH

Singers and wind players must distinguish between the punctuation of phrasing and the physical necessity of breathing. Both are differently conditioned, though they often coincide. As a rule, a phrase has the length of its breath. But with singers, more so than with wind players, phrasing is a complex technical problem. It depends on both individual skill and individual physique. Phrases to be sung are usually as long as the verbal clauses of the text, but in a slow tempo they are sometimes longer than a singer's breath. If breathing is unavoidable at a point where a comma would be out of place, intelligent musicians know how to breathe imperceptibly.

Breath control is indispensable. A long breath is a great advantage to a singer who understands how to use it for sensitive phrasing. He will sometimes forgo taking breath for the sake of a melodic line's continuity. Leonora's recitative from *Fidelio* may serve as an example. A breath after 'Farbenbogen' is certainly permissible, yet there were (and, I hope, still are) singers capable of singing the whole passage in one breath, thus successfully conveying the picture of the rainbow of hope that Beethoven had in his mind.

Beethoven, Fidelio, *Op. 72, Leonora's aria*

## ARTICULATION

Notes that form a motif, an upbeat, or a distinct rhythmic pattern should be joined by rhythmic means (e.g., *legato* or *rubato obbligato*) or graded dynamics (e.g., accentuation). Often, however, clear articulation will suffice for distinguishing a motif.

Articulation, i.e., the exact hitting of a note (cf. Chapter II/2A, pp. 38–47), is the most subtle means of phrasing and can, on a small scale, replace accents as well as punctuation —and for reasons of artistic economy, the subtle means is preferable. By holding stronger methods in reserve, a wider scope is secured. Accents are articulate by nature, but articulation itself need not be accentuated. At the opening of the G minor symphony, for instance (cf. Ex. 42), the first quaver of the *appoggiatura* motif must be clearly attacked, but, of course, not accentuated. The motif's crotchet should also be articulated, but accentuated only in the third bar.

It is a widespread bad habit to place an accent on every

note that needs distinct articulation. 'Strong' beats should be articulated, but not, as a rule, accentuated. The Andante of Mozart's Symphony in E flat, for instance, needs no accent whatsoever, only one stress (rhythmical!), and highly differentiated articulations.

Articulation makes its point without undue emphasis, but with discrimination. In the Minuet of the G minor symphony (48), while commas are required before the crotchet up-beats in bars 3 and 6, distinct articulations suffice later on when the three-bar model (cf. Chapter III, p. 99) is reduced to one bar (bars 8, 9 and 10) and finally compressed into single crotchets (bars 11 and 12). The second beats of bars 9 and 10 must be clearly articulated, and the same applies to each of the five descending crotchets in bars 11 and 12.

## STACCATO

The dynamic character of the symphony's Minuet is *f*. Thus the *staccato* crotchets of the last bars are, of necessity, accentuated. *Staccato* in *f* makes for an explosive sound, a consequence of the gaps between the short notes. But *staccato* is not usually accentuated. The main function of *staccato* is clear articulation of swift, especially repeated, notes. Its other important functions are: to stress the rhythmic character of a shape (long notes are essentially melodic); to make transparent an accompaniment or a polyphonic texture; to distinguish a note or group of notes from the surroundings. *Staccato* has a sonority of its own, a definite quality of colour which, though it differs from instrument to instrument, makes always for dryness of tone and clarity of the notes.

The performer should be capable of the widest possible range of both *staccatos* (cf. Chapter II/2A, pp. 44–46) and articulations. In this respect, the piano has great advantages over other instruments. Its perfect articulation gives the skilful performer a wide scope not only in grading the shortness of *staccatos*, but also in colouring them diversely by

169

way of touch, textural balance and pedalling. Diversity of *staccatos* is not solely a matter of technique; its primary source is imagination—imagination, inspired by the shape of the music.

The *staccato* of string instruments is less satisfactory. *Staccato* notes, in particular, easily become automatic—all the notes sound the same whatever their individual place in the phrase. If *staccato* has a purely colouristic function, as in Mendelssohn's *Midsummer Night's Dream* overture, no elaborate phrasing is wanted. But if motifs and phrases are under development, *staccato* becomes a means of phrasing and must be differentiated. In the scherzo from the sixth symphony of Tchaikovsky, the *staccatos* of the melody should be phrased. The beats, especially the first and third

*Tchaikovsky, Symphony No. 6 in B minor, 3rd mvt.*

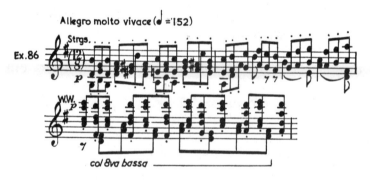

of each bar, must be decisively articulated. In the second bar, the *staccatos* should grow shorter while the melodic line rises. When, in the third bar, the woodwind enters, the melodic structure becomes uniform and needs less articulation.

*Crescendo* and *diminuendo* change the sonority of *staccato* notes. Increased tone volume makes the notes sound longer; in order to maintain the same brevity, the *staccato* must become shorter. In *diminuendo*, on the other hand, the notes sound shorter, and this will often coincide with the diminishing character of the music.

The second subject of the *Jupiter* symphony includes a variety of *staccato* notes which should not be played uniformly. The D in the fourth bar is the shortest—it ends a phrase.

*Mozart, Symphony No. 41 in C (Jupiter), K.551, 1st mvt.*

Thus the following quaver rest is prolonged and allows for semi-articulation of the subsequent *legato* D. The notes C and B in the fifth bar and again in the eleventh, have greater structural significance than the earlier *staccato*

notes; they belong to motif (b) which is subsequently developed, until, in the twelfth bar, the quavers become *staccato* crotchets. These points may seem minute, but they are by no means negligible—the character of the theme is at stake.

The *staccatos* in the codetta of the same movement are still more subtly differentiated. Phrase (A), which is played

*Mozart, Symphony No. 41 in C, 1st mvt.*

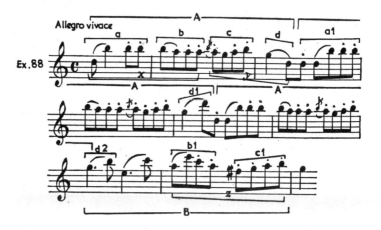

three times (with slight variations), is a closely woven unit. After the leap D–B, the melodic line moves downwards. The principal notes are B–A–G–D, each of which is, the first time, non-*staccato*. The phrase begins and ends *legato*, in disjunct motion. In contrast, the centre of the phrase contains chiefly *staccato* notes, but the shortness of the *staccatos* differs. If, for convenience's sake, we divide the phrase into the particles (a), (b), (c), and (d)—which could hardly be called motifs—we have three groups of *staccato* notes. In (a) and (b), the *staccato* notes merely repeat the preceding *legato* crotchet and quaver (respectively), and should be given less prominence (i.e., shortness) than those of the third group. None the less, the *staccatos* after a quaver (b) must be made shorter than those after a crotchet (a). In (c) the *staccato*

172

notes are melodically differentiated and, after a short *appoggiatura*, should be the shortest—*staccatissimo*, in fact.

The six *staccato* notes in phrase (B) are not as short as those of particle (c), but shorter than those of (b). Phrase (B), which completes the rhythmic structure of eight bars, contrasts with phrase (A) in melodic, harmonic, textural and, above all, rhythmic respects. Not only because it begins on a downbeat. While the particles of (A) form a single, closely knit unit, (B) consists of two motifs, ($d^2$) and (z), grouped into three units—two of half a bar and one of one bar. Motif ($d^2$) is a variation of (d), (z) a variation of (b) and (c) combined. In phrase (B), which dominates the development and lead-back sections of the movement, the particles are grouped differently from (A). While the *staccatos* of (A) help to differentiate the line of an integrated unit, the succession of six *staccatos* in (B) contributes to the integration of a shape that is more loosely built. There is a further distinction between the *staccato* notes of the phrases. In (A) the movement's trend is towards the crotchet G, which is the centre of the shape. In (B) the melody centres on the first note A of motif (z), and the subsequent *staccato* notes do not drive forward, but move at a fairly steady pace. *Staccatos* are not ornaments, architectural finials, as it were, but part and parcel of the rhythm. They are a means of phrasing, which should register certain details of the structure in adequately graded proportions.

## STRESS

The performer should be aware of the rhythmic character of the notes, that is, of their actual length as distinct from their time value; he should know that only *legato* notes are sustained to their full value. The indications (–) and *ten.*, as well as *stacc.*, are only signposts, and are often lacking where the structure requires sustaining. They are not indicated, for instance, at the end of the 'March of the Priests', from Mozart's *Magic Flute*, where the surprising interrupted cadences on the chords of the submediant and subdominant (cf. Ex. 89 at $x$) need the emphasis of a slight prolongation.

Mozart, The Magic Flute, 2nd act, sc. I

Ex. 89

Accents on the chords are out of the question. They would impair the melodic climax of three successive phrases, whose initial notes, C, D, and F, are marked *sfp*. The cadences of the three phrases are all *diminuendo*. Phrase-ends should not be clipped. It is a bad habit, especially among woodwind players, to shorten the last note. Often an otherwise beautifully played melody is spoilt in this way and its character distorted. The end of a phrase is to be phrased according

174

to its own structure as well as in anticipation of what comes after. 'Phrasing-off' is better achieved by dynamic means (*dim.*) than by 'clipping'. A melody is rhythmically defined not only by the length of the notes but also by the gaps, i.e., the 'air', between them, be the notes *staccato* or detached.

*Beethoven, Symphony No. 7 in A, Op. 92, 2nd mvt.*

There is some air between any two chords. Though the movement of the Allegretto from Beethoven's seventh symphony (Ex. 90) is strictly in time, the duration of the notes varies. The first (*ten.*) is almost a full crotchet; the *staccato* quavers are not very short, about as short as semi-quavers, and the subsequent crotchets a little longer than quavers. The stress on the first note, though without accent, marks the centre of gravity of the two-bar motif. If it is not sustained, the two *staccato* quavers will be felt as an upbeat. The motif, as a result, will centre on the second bar and thus completely destroy the heavy character of the melody.

It may be taken, with a grain of salt, that the length of a note depends upon its importance within the phrase. The centre of gravity is often emphasized by a stress, and a shifting of the stress changes the character of a phrase. In the Andante of Mozart's E flat symphony, it makes all the difference if the first crotchet is well sustained or not, or worse, if a stress is applied to the crotchet of the second bar instead. I believe that the calmness of the four-bar clause is best conveyed if all accents are avoided, but the crotchets of the first and fourth bars a little stressed.

In vocal music the length of a syllable often modifies the note-value and provides a stress. In the melody from Weber's *Der Freischütz*, the A♮ on the long syllable *Wäl-*

Weber, Der Freischütz, *1st act, Max's aria*

must be duly stressed and the line rise thereafter in a *diminuendo*; otherwise the short syllable *-der* on the higher note will be obtrusively emphasized. Owing to its bright colour the high register of the voice is very emphatic and can sometimes produce a dynamic climax where one is not wanted.

# INDEX

INDEX

Rhythm—*contd.*
 syncopations, 43–4
 *tenuto*, 44–5
 upbeats, 41–3
Rhythmic structure, 91–3, 98–103, 105
*Ritardando*, 50, 150–4, 157–9
*Ritenuto*, 152–3
*Ritornello*, 122
*Rosenkavalier, Der* (R. Strauss).
 143, *144*
*Rubato*, 39, 48–50, 142, 164;
 *obbligato*, 39, 49, 129

*St. John Passion* (Bach), *106*, 106–7, 159
*St. Matthew Passion* (Bach), *29*, 146
Schnabel, Artur, quoted, 45
Schoenberg, Arnold, 23;
 on dissonance, 33
 on dynamics, 61, 63
 on 'extended tonality', 106
 on metronome figures, 53
 on rhythmic symmetry, 103
 *Five Orchestral Pieces*, 68
 *Harmonielehre*, 31
 *Models for Beginners in Composition*, 86n.
 *Piano Piece, Op. 11, No. 2, 119*
 *Pierrot lunaire*, *119*, 119–20, *141*, 141–3
 *Serenade*, *46*, 100–1, *102*
 *Structural Functions of Harmony*, 107n.
Schubert, Franz:
 *Moment Musical* see *Moment Musical*
 *Piano Sonata in A*, 88, *89*
 *Piano Sonata in D*, 87, *88*, 104n.
 *Piano Sonata in E flat*, *153*, 153–4
 *Symphony No. 7 in C*, 99–100, *100*, 163
 *Unfinished Symphony*, 85
Schumann, Clara, 53

Schumann, Robert, 53;
 *Der arme Peter II*, *131*, 131–4
 *Fantasia in C major*, 59
 *Träumerei*, *123*, 123–5
Sentences, 91, 93–5
*Serenade* (Schoenberg), *46*, 101, *102*
*Sforzato*, 61
Shapes in music, 72–80, 83–6, 102–3;
 of closing sections, 85
 of introductions, 84
 of principal sections, 84
 of subsidiary sections, 84–5
 of transitions and episodes, 85
*Siegfried* (Wagner) as example of:
 colour, 117
 harmony, *36*, *105*, 105–6, 109
*Staccato*, 45, 169–73;
 of piano music, 169–70
 of strings, 170
Strauss, Johann:
 *Blue Danube*, 146, *147*
 *Viennese Waltz*, 161
Strauss, Richard:
 quoted, 52
 *Rosenkavalier, Der*, 143, *145*
 *Till Eulenspiegel*, *160*
Stravinsky, Igor, 61;
 *Orpheus*, 100, *101*, 159
Stress (*see also* Accentuation), 173–6
Strings:
 *staccato* of, 170
 timbre and colour of, 65
*Structural Functions of Harmony* (Schoenberg), 107n.
Structure (*see also* Texture), 69–125;
 antecedent and consequent, 81–2, 101
 beginning and ending, 70–2
 character and, 122–6
 closing sections, 85
 colour as a feature of, 116–20
 density of, 83, 102–3, 161

181